BTEC National Travel and Tourism

Book 3

Specialist units

Derek Brickell

Andy Kerr

Victoria Lindsay

Carol Spencer

Diane Sutherland

Jon Sutherland

A PEARSON COMPANY

Contents

How to use this book

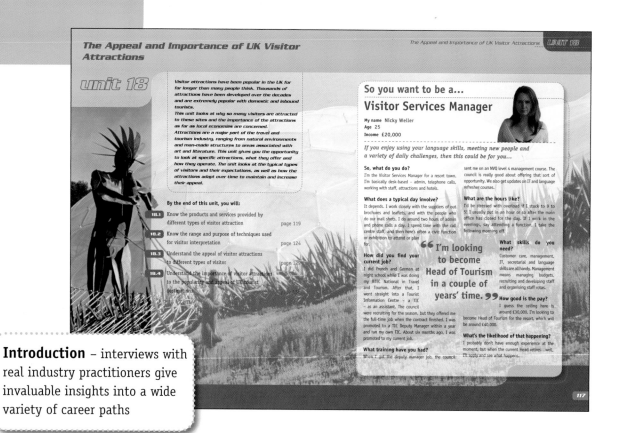

Introduction – interviews with real industry practitioners give invaluable insights into a wide variety of career paths

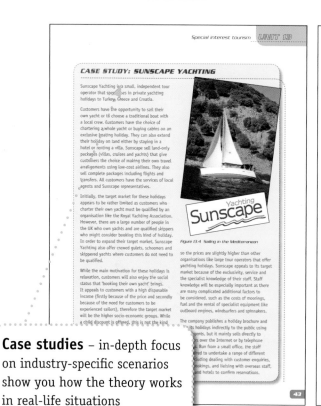

Case studies – in-depth focus on industry-specific scenarios show you how the theory works in real-life situations

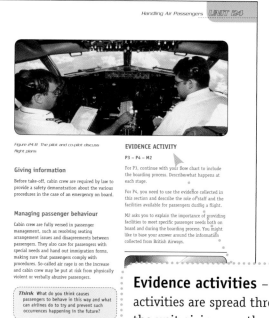

Evidence activities – short activities are spread throughout the unit giving you the opportunity to practise your achievement of the grading criteria in small steps

Grading criteria – learning outcomes and grading criteria are located at the beginning of every unit, so you know right from the start what you need to do to achieve a pass, merit or distinction

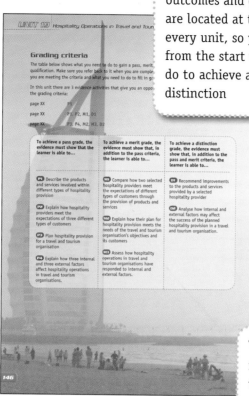

Think – questions help you reflect on your learning and to think about how it could be applied to real-life working practice

Research Tips – direct you to useful websites and key organisations to help you take your study further

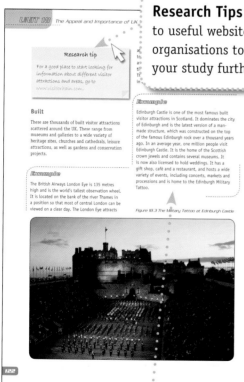

Examples – industry-specific examples show you what the theory looks like in practice

Key words – easy to understand definitions of key industry terms

Track your progress

This master grid can be used as a study aid. You can track your progress by ticking the level you achieve. The relevant grading criteria can also be found at the start of each unit.

To achieve a pass grade the evidence must show that the learner is able to...	To achieve a merit grade the evidence must show that, in addition to the pass criteria, the learner is able to...	To achieve a distinction grade the evidence must show that, in addition to the pass and merit criteria, the learner is able to...
Unit 10		
P1 Explain the development and structure of the cruise sector	**M1** Compare and contrast the routes and ship facilities of two different types of cruises	**D1** Analyse opportunities for future growth within the current cruise sector
P2 Describe the facilities and cruises available from different types of ships	**M2** Explain how the selected cruises appeal to the customer	**D2** Make realistic recommendations about how to maximise positive and minimise negative impacts of cruising.
P3 Select appropriate cruises that would appeal to two different types of customers	**M3** Explain the impacts of cruising on a selected cruise area.	
P4 Describe four cruise areas of the world		
P5 Describe the impacts of cruising on one cruise area, its gateway ports and ports of call		
P6 Describe three different employment opportunities available in the cruise sector.		
Unit 13		
P1 Describe the development of the relationship between special interests and tourism	**M1** Explain how two relationships between special interests and tourism have developed	**D1** Assess the current market for special interest tourism, identify gaps in provision and suggest potential new products
P2 Describe three industry factors and three participant factors that affect participation in passive, active and adventure special interest tourism	**M2** Analyse how two key factors have affected participation in each of passive, active and adventure special interest tourism	**D2** Evaluate the provision for a specific special interest and justify recommendations for development.
P3 Describe the nature of activities in special interest tourism	**M3** Analyse the tourism provision for a specific special interest.	
P4 Identify and show 20 key worldwide locations including passive, active and adventure activities (four should be in the UK)		
P5 Describe the tourism provision for a specific special interest, including locations and special requirements.		

To achieve a pass grade the evidence must show that the learner is able to...	To achieve a merit grade the evidence must show that, in addition to the pass criteria, the learner is able to...	To achieve a distinction grade the evidence must show that, in addition to the pass and merit criteria, the learner is able to...
Unit 14		
P1 Describe the roles and responsibilities for three different categories of holiday representatives	**M1** Compare the roles and responsibilities for two categories of holiday representatives	**D1** Analyse how the roles and responsibilities of the holiday representative can contribute to the overall holiday experience
P2 Identify and explain the legal responsibilities of holiday representatives in four different holiday situations	**M2** Demonstrate effective social, customer service and selling skills when delivering a transfer speech and welcome meeting	**D2** Consistently project a confident, professional image when dealing with customers in different situations.
P3 Describe the role played by holiday representatives in creating a safe and healthy holiday environment	**M3** Deal effectively with customers in different situations and accurately complete all relevant documentation.	
P4 Use social, customer service and selling skills to deliver an arrival transfer speech and plan and deliver a welcome meeting, completing appropriate documentation		
P5 Use social and customer service skills to deal with customers in different situations, completing appropriate documentation.		
Unit 15		
P1 Describe passenger transport operations within the UK	**M1** Explain how the UK passenger transport sector responds to developments and factors	**D1** Evaluate the extent to which passenger transport in the UK supports the economic growth of tourism, making reference to specific examples
P2 Describe three significant development and three factors affecting and influencing passenger transport within the UK	**M2** Recommend and justify realistic measures to enhance relationships between passenger transport and the UK travel and tourism industry	**D2** Evaluate the contribution of passenger transport provision to the popularity and appeal in a specific tourist destination, making recommendations for improvements.
P3 Explain the relationships between UK passenger transport networks and the travel and tourism industry	**M3** Assess the effectiveness of passenger transport in a specific tourist destination and the effect on its popularity and appeal to tourists.	
P4 Describe five types of transport provision in a specific UK tourist destination		
P5 Explain how passenger transport provision can influence the popularity and appeal of tourist destinations.		

To achieve a pass grade the evidence must show that the learner is able to...	To achieve a merit grade the evidence must show that, in addition to the pass criteria, the learner is able to...	To achieve a distinction grade the evidence must show that, in addition to the pass and merit criteria, the learner is able to...
Unit 18		
P1 Describe the products and services provided by one built and one natural visitor attraction	**M1** Analyse how effectively the products, services and interpretation techniques of a built and a natural attraction are used to meet the needs of three different types of visitors	**D1** Make realistic and justified recommendations for improvements to the products, services and interpretation techniques used by a selected built or natural attraction to meet the needs of different types of visitors
P2 Describe the techniques used for visitor interpretation at one built and one natural visitor attraction	**M2** Explain how one built or natural attraction could adapt to appeal to a wider range of visitor types	**D2** Evaluate the success of visitor attractions to the popularity and appeal of a destination or area, making recommendations for improvement.
P3 Explain the appeal of one selected natural and one built visitor attraction to three different types of visitors	**M3** Explain the impact visitor attractions have had on the popularity and appeal of a destination or area.	
P4 Explain why visitor attractions are important to UK tourism.		
Unit 19		
P1 Describe the products and services involved within different types of hospitality provision	**M1** Compare how two selected hospitality providers meet the expectations of different types of customers through the provision of products and services	**D1** Recommend improvements to the products and services provided by a selected hospitality provider
P2 Explain how hospitality providers meet the expectations of three different types of customers	**M2** Explain how the plan for hospitality provision meets the needs of the travel and tourism organisation's objectives and its customers	**D2** Analyse how internal and external factors may affect the success of the planned hospitality provision in a travel and tourism organisation.
P3 Plan hospitality provision for a travel and tourism organisation	**M3** Assess how hospitality operations in travel and tourism organisations have responded to internal and external factors.	
P4 Explain how three internal and three external factors affect hospitality operations in travel and tourism organisations.		
Unit 24		
P1 Describe the options available to customers when travelling to and from airports and between terminals	**M1** Compare the facilities available at two different airports for passengers travelling to and from the airports and during the embarkation process	**D1** Evaluate the effectiveness of processes for handling passengers during embarkation at a specific airport, making justified recommendations for improvement
P2 Describe the process for embarkation for all passengers and the role that airport and airline staff have during the embarkation of customers	**M2** Explain the importance of providing facilities to meet specific passenger needs both onboard and during the boarding process	**D2** Analyse the effectiveness of disembarkation processes at a UK airport.
P3 Describe the boarding process	**M3** Explain the importance of effective disembarkation processes at UK airports.	
P4 Describe the role of staff and the facilities available for customers during a flight		
P5 Describe the disembarkation and transit process at UK airports.		

Research Skills

Before you start your research project you need to know where to find information and the guidelines you must follow.

Types of information

Primary Sources

This is information you have gathered yourself, through surveys, interviews, photos or observation. Ensure that you ask the appropriate questions and people. You must get permission before including someone's photo or interview in your work.

Secondary Sources

This is information produced by somebody else, including information from the Internet, books, magazines, databases and television. You need to be sure that your secondary source is reliable if you are going to use the information.

Information sources

The Internet

The Internet is a useful research tool, but, not all the information you find will be. When using the Internet ask yourself if you can trust the information you find.

> Acknowledge your source! When quoting from the internet always include author name (if known)/document title/URL web address/date site was accessed.

Books, Magazines and Newspapers

Information in newspapers and magazines is up to date and usually researched thoroughly. Books have a longer shelf life than newspapers so make sure you use the most recent edition.

> Acknowledge your source! When quoting from books, magazines, journal or papers, always include author name/ title of publication/publisher/year of publication.

Broadcast Media

Television and radio broadcast current news stories and the information should be accurate. Be aware that some programmes offer personal opinions as well as facts.

Plagiarism

Plagiarism is including in your own work extracts or ideas from another source without acknowledging its origins. If you use any material from other sources you must acknowledge it. This includes the work of fellow students.

Storing Information

Keep a record of all the information you gather. Record details of book titles, author names, page references, web addresses (URLs) and contact details of interviewees. Accurate, accessible records will help you acknowledge sources and find information quickly.

Internet Dos and Don'ts

Do

- check information against other sources

- keep a record of where you found information and acknowledge the source

- be aware that not all sites are genuine or trustworthy.

Don't Ø

- assume all the information on the Internet is accurate and up to date

- copy material from websites without checking whether permission from the copyright holder is required

- give personal information to people you meet on the Internet.

Investigating the cruise sector

unit 10

The cruise industry is one of the largest growth sectors in the travel and tourism industry. The number of cruises taken has risen by over 32% in the past 5 years compared to 16% for land-based holidays. The cruise sector will be worth £1.8 billion by 2008 and the industry expects an average of 2 million cruise passengers each year by 2010. North America is the largest cruising market, with the UK in second place. With the industry growing so rapidly, the opportunities to work in the cruise sector are numerous, either on land or at sea. Once at sea, the members of a ship's crew have the opportunity to travel the world. Shore-side jobs also offer a range of different positions, including working face-to-face with customers and behind the scenes roles in brochure creation or staff training.

By the end of this unit, you will:

So you want to be a...

Ship's Purser

My name Andy Wilson

Age 28

Income £33,000 tax free, paid in US Dollars

If you can think on your feet, like to travel and enjoy a challenge then maybe you should take to the sea...

What do you do?

I work onboard a cruise ship, dealing with passenger enquiries, payments and money exchange.

What responsibilities do you have?

When passengers board the ship, I'm involved in the meet and greet process and deal with customer enquiries. Whilst onboard passengers may need assistance with a range of different things, including information about the ship and the ports we visit. I exchange money, process passport details and billing arrangements. I take their credit card details at the start and sort out any billing discrepancies before they leave the ship.

How did you get the job?

I did a Travel and Tourism GCSE and then a BTEC National Diploma at college. I worked in a travel agency for some years to gain customer service experience.

How did you find your current job?

It was advertised on the Internet. I had two interviews: one with the agency that vets applicants applying for cruise jobs, and the other with the cruise company.

What training did you get?

Mostly on the job. I started work the day I flew out to join the ship – I was given a uniform and started there and then. At first I worked on the purser's desk, with a more experienced person, during the quiet times. I had to complete a survival course before I joined the ship and then did emergency drill training on board.

What are the hours like?

I usually work an 8-hour shift, either from 7 a.m. to 3 p.m. or from 3 p.m. to 11 p.m. When it's busy, we sometimes do a split shift to cover morning and evening rushes. I get a full day off every two weeks.

> **" I would like to be a Chief Purser one day "**

What skills do you need?

My experience in customer services helped. You need to be organised and deal with issues as they come up.

How good is the pay?

The basic is very good and it's tax free! When I'm on board I get accommodation, food and uniform included. However, when I'm not on board, I don't get paid.

What about the future?

I'd like to do this job for a few more years and then look for promotion. There are opportunities to progress to Senior Purser and then, maybe one day, Chief Purser.

Grading criteria

The table below shows what you need to do to gain a pass, merit or distinction in this part of the qualification. Make sure you refer back to it when you are completing work so that you can judge whether you are meeting the criteria and what you need to do to fill in gaps in your knowledge or experience.

In this unit there are 4 evidence activities that give you an opportunity to demonstrate your achievement of the grading criteria:

page 20	P1, P2, M1, D1
page 23	P3, M2
page 30	P4, P5, M3, D2
page 33	P6

To achieve a pass grade the evidence must show that the learner is able to...	To achieve a merit grade the evidence must show that, in addition to the pass criteria, the learner is able to...	To achieve a distinction grade the evidence must show that, in addition to the pass and merit criteria, the learner is able to...
P1 Explain the development and structure of the cruise sector	**M1** Compare and contrast the routes and ship facilities of two different types of cruises	**D1** Analyse opportunities for future growth within the current cruise sector
P2 Describe the facilities and cruises available from different types of ships	**M2** Explain how the selected cruises appeal to the customer	**D2** Make realistic recommendations about how to maximise positive and minimise negative impacts of cruising.
P3 Select appropriate cruises that would appeal to two different types of customers	**M3** Explain the impacts of cruising on a selected cruise area.	
P4 Describe four cruise areas of the world		
P5 Describe the impacts of cruising on one cruise area, its gateway ports and ports of call		
P6 Describe three different employment opportunities available in the cruise sector.		

10.1 *Understand the development and structure of the cruise sector*

DEVELOPMENT

A cruise ship is a passenger ship that sails from one port to another. Given the amount of time spent onboard, the ship's facilities and atmosphere are often as important to the passenger as the ports visited.

Some of the first cruise liners were transatlantic ships that were used for freight. As cruises became more popular, some of the freight and cargo ships were transformed into passenger-only ships. This was done by changing the ship's interior.

The first companies to offer cruises on purpose-built cruise ships were the P&O Line (the Peninsula and Oriental Steam Navigation Company), which ran ships from the UK to Europe and to the Far East, and the Black Ball Line, which operated transatlantic ships from New York to Liverpool.

The first cruise ships often divided their facilities according to the amount of money that passengers had spent. Certain luxurious restaurants with outside areas were only made available to first class passengers. Cruise ships were seen as a form of transportation, but also as a luxury, relaxing holiday. They were considered to be expensive and a status symbol for rich passengers.

During the First and Second World Wars, cruise ships were used to transport troops around the world. Ships remained popular until the first transatlantic crossing by aeroplane. The plane was not only a faster way to cross the Atlantic, but it was also a status symbol that was more prestigious than cruising. The growth of the aviation industry led to a decline in the popularity of cruise ships both for holidays and as a form of transport.

The cruise industry undertook a re-packaging of cruise ships during the 1980s and 1990s and this led to a renewed interest in cruising, although the holidays were still seen as a luxury product. During the 1990s, several operators changed their approach to cruising and a number of less luxurious, cheaper cruises were offered to passengers who had previously not even considered booking a cruise.

Recently cruise ships have become larger, providing all of their passengers with a wide range of facilities. The original class system has been removed and there is a less formal atmosphere onboard many ships.

The cruise industry does not only cover sea and ocean-going vessels, but it also includes river boats and canal holidays. Canal boats that are now used for holidays were originally designed to transport cargo like coal around the canals and rivers of the UK. There are a range of different sizes of river boats and they were originally used as ferries for local people to get from one location to another.

Key words

Cruise ship – a passenger ship that sails from one port to another
Freight – goods that are transported from one place to another

Research tip

Ask members of your family what they think about cruises to gain an impression about this type of holiday.

Think Do you think that people still regard a cruise as a luxury holiday?

STRUCTURE

Cruise operators and links with other sectors

Cruise operators own and run cruise ships. Some large operators like Norwegian Cruise Line, Carnival and Costa own several ships, but medium-sized operators such as the Clipper Group own two or three ships and smaller specialist operators may only own and operate one ship.

Most cruise operators sell cabins directly to passengers over the telephone, through newspaper adverts or over the Internet. These can be cruise-only holidays or they may also include flights and the transfer from the airport to the embarkation port at the start of the cruise and from the ship to the airport at the disembarkation point at the end of the cruise.

In addition, cruise operators will also allocate a certain number of cabins to tour operators who sell the cruises as a package holiday or as part of a tour or resort stay.

Example

Thomson offers Cruise and Stay holidays, which include 7 nights in a hotel and 7 nights on a cruise around the Mediterranean.

Given that booking a cruise can be complicated, cruise companies publish their own brochures and often use travel agents to sell and book the cruises. The travel agents earn commission on each cruise that they sell. Other operators use their own specially trained staff to sell directly to their customers by taking bookings over the Internet or telephone.

Key words

Embarkation port – the port where a passenger joins the ship at the start of their cruise
Disembarkation point – the port where the passenger leaves the ship at the end of their cruise

Tour operators and integration

Some tour operators own their own cruise ships and sell package holidays through their own travel agents. These holidays include flights with their own airline and accommodation in hotels that they own. Tour operators that do this are integrated and they own a number of different types of travel and tourism organisations. The advantage of a tour operator owning their own ship is that they can arrange the on-board facilities such as entertainment and menus to meet the needs of their target market. They can also choose the embarkation and disembarkation points to match their flight schedules and run itineraries that they feel will appeal to their customers.

Recently, several tour operators have found it too expensive to own their own ships. Instead, they have entered into a number of different arrangements with cruise operators.

Further information about tour operators can be found in Book 1, Unit 12.

Example

First Choice runs a joint cruising venture with Royal Caribbean Cruises.

Example

Other specialist tour operators such as Nobel Caledonian charter a ship for a particular week or cruise and fill all of the cabins with their customers for that cruise.

Figure 10.1 The Thomson cruise ship Destiny

Regulatory bodies

The International Maritime Organization (or IMO) was founded in 1959 and is the United Nations organisation responsible for shipping and the seas. It is involved in developing and implementing regulations for cruise ships, including safety and environmental issues. The IMO also sets standards for the training of seafarers and crew onboard ships.

The ISPS Code (International Ship and Port Facility Security Code) provides regulations about the security of ships and ports, including gangway procedures, the use of **ID cards**, procedures for X-raying luggage and guidelines for the searching and running of background checks on passengers.

Research tip

Use the IMO website www.imo.org to find out more about the IMO. The newsroom facility provides up-to-date cruise and shipping news.

Think Using the IMO newsroom link, what are the current hot topics?

The International Council of Cruise Lines merged with the Cruise Lines International Association in 2006 and the joint organisation is now called the Cruise Lines International Association.

This is an American organisation through which cruise operators work together to promote cruises, raise the safety and security standards onboard ships and provide customers with up-to-date information about the industry. The website www.cruising.org offers information about their members, which include cruise operators, travel agencies and any organisations that provide services to the cruise industry, such as ports and excursion operators. The website also provides statistics about the cruise industry and profiles of cruise ships and cruise lines.

Cruise UK is an organisation funded by VisitBritain that aims to develop the cruise industry in the UK. Its aims include increasing the number of ports in the UK that are frequented by cruise ships, as well as the different types of ships that cruise around the UK.

Research tip

Use an Internet search engine and cruise holiday brochures to research which UK ports currently receive cruise ships.

Think Why do you think that people would want to visit the UK by cruise ship?

Key words

ID cards – cards given to passengers in order for them to charge purchases to their cabin and also to identify them as passengers to the ship's crew

Figure 10.2 The 'captain' and a passenger enjoy a photo opportunity

10.2 Know different types of cruises, ships and the facilities they offer

TYPES OF CRUISES

Cruise ships vary in size and also in terms of the facilities that they offer. Some ships will only cruise around a specific area or region, due to the size of the ship or the fact that the type of ship is only suitable for that region. Only ships that are ice breakers can cruise around some areas of the Arctic and Antarctic. Flat-bottomed boats must be used in some rivers and canals as the water is not very deep.

Fly-cruises

Most cruises involve a flight to join the ship and this type of holiday is therefore called a fly-cruise. One-way flights and cruises back to the home country could also be considered a fly-cruise.

Example

Cunard Cruises offer a fly-cruise holiday that includes a flight to New York and a cruise back to Southampton on the Queen Mary.

Round the world cruises

Larger cruise ships will often undertake a round the world cruise during the winter months. These often begin and end in the Mediterranean. The ship cruises to ports in Africa and Asia before visiting some areas of Australia and crossing the Indian and Atlantic Oceans to South and North America. Large continents like Africa and South America are crossed using canals or large rivers like the Suez Canal in Egypt.

Customers can choose to book a segment of a world cruise, such as the voyage from Singapore to Australia, or they can choose to book the whole cruise. Round the world cruises normally take seven months and the full cruise can cost £23,000 for 100 nights.

Mini-cruises

There are normally two different types of these short cruises. The first type allows tourists to visit an area of interest.

The second type of mini-cruise departs from a port near to the passenger's home and offers them a taster of the cruise experience, allowing them to sample cruise life before booking a longer holiday.

Example

Thomson offers a one-night taster cruise that departs from Harwich and ends in Southampton. While onboard, passengers enjoy a five-course meal and all the entertainment normally associated with a cruise ship.

River cruises

Most river cruises use river boats, which are the only boats that can cruise in this area. They are sometimes special to the region, such as the paddle steamers on the Mississippi River. River cruises normally have fixed itineraries and embarkation and disembarkation points. River cruises can be either up or down river and the only difference between the two is the order in which the attractions are visited.

Figure 10.3 A paddle steamer on the Mississippi River

In order to limit some of these impacts, the Florida-Caribbean Cruise Association together with local groups is implementing an environmental code of good practice for cruise operators. This includes guidelines about environmentally sound cruising, the sharing of best practice and rewards for the use of recycling, clean technologies and a good environmental record. Attempts are also being made to increase the financial gain from the cruise industry and to use this money to support local projects like schools and clinics.

3. Transport

The impacts of transportation are mainly evident around the ports and tourist attractions visited. In order to accommodate the large numbers of passengers, additional access roads around ports and airports have been built. There is more traffic on the roads, not only due to the coaches used for the passengers, but also because of the supply lorries carrying food and drink to the ships and water containers delivering fresh water. The increase in traffic has led to air pollution and roadside littering.

This impact is difficult to control, although some destinations like Anguilla have limited the number of arriving passengers to 200 per day. Therefore, these destinations only receive smaller, more exclusive ships that require less tourist infrastructure.

4. Use and consumption

At each port, the ship will load fresh food, clean water and drinks onboard to ensure that they have sufficient supplies for the passengers and crew. The food and drink required may not be available in the local area and many of these products are bought in from overseas. In this case, the majority of the money earned from the sale of goods to the ship is spent on buying the original imported produce or transportation costs.

Other supply needs, such as fresh water, are provided locally by the destinations. Supplying ships with fresh water and produce can cause a strain on the existing local resources. Destinations sometimes experience water shortages as the fresh water has been used to supply a ship as opposed to being kept for local use. Water, gas, fuel and electricity are also used while a ship is in port.

In order to limit these impacts, ports are trying to encourage ships to invest in modern technologies like solar power. They are also encouraging the use of local produce in the menus and restaurants onboard.

5. Disposal

Disposal issues focus on the destruction of the ship's waste products, including garbage, water and sewage. The IMO has specific rules and regulations about the offloading and disposal of waste. Although ships are allowed to burn some garbage onboard and dump clean waste water into remote areas of deep sea, the majority of waste products are offloaded in port. This can cause additional stress on the domestic facilities and some of the larger ports have built specific sewage plants and waste disposal complexes in order to deal with the large amounts of waste products generated by the visiting ships.

Figure 10.9 Impacts on ports of call can be varied

ITINERARIES

A ship's itinerary provides information about where the ship is going to visit. When choosing their cruise, customers will consider this information in detail as it provides an overview of the cruise.

Ports of call

These are the places where the cruise ship will stop. They are normally selected because they offer something interesting to the passengers or allow them to visit areas of special interest. Sometimes the ports and cities visited are not the main attraction. Naples is the port closest to Pompeii and the port is therefore used to allow passengers to visit the ancient ruins.

Gateway airports

In terms of cruising, a gateway airport is the main airport that is nearest to the embarkation and disembarkation port. Some cruises are circular and passengers will therefore fly in and out of the same gateway airport. Other passengers will use different arrival and departure gateway airports.

Facilities at the port

The facilities available in ports may make an impact on a customer's choice of cruise. Some ports offer shops and restaurants specifically for cruise passengers.

Example

Piraeus, the port in Athens, is close to the airport and has a range of facilities for passengers. It has the capacity to accommodate large cruise ships.

Excursions available

Many people book cruises as they wish to visit a particular area or visitor attraction. In order to ensure that they visit these sites, passengers choose a ship that includes them in the itinerary and they may pre-book an excursion.

Helsinki, Finland
Sunrise: 03.08

Thursday 03 July, 2003
Sunset: 22.40

06:30	Early risers' Coffee is ready in the Main Lounge
07:30–09:30	Breakfast Buffet is served in the Dining Room
09:45	MANDATORY LIFE BOARD DRILL. Bring the life vest from your cabin and come to your Muster Station on the Lido Deck. Attendance of this drill is required by international law. Crew will be standing by to help you locate your muster station. Those in port side cabins meet under the port side lifeboat, starboard side cabins meet under the starboard side lifeboat)
10:00	Hot Bouillon is served in the Lido Deck
10:30	'St. Petersburg: Peter The Great's Three Purposes' a talk by Peter Unwin in the Lounge. Followed by a short information briefing on our day in Helsinki.
12:00	Sea Cloud II comes alongside in Helsinki
12:30	Buffet Lunch will be served in the Dining Lounge
14:00	Departure of the afternoon tour. Our tour today will be on foot, and will include the Summer Market, the President's Palace and the impressive architecture of Senate Square. Either return with our guides to the ship at around 16:00, or continue to explore Helsinki independently
16:00	Afternoon Tea is available in the Lido Deck
18:15	A Concert of Russian Music by Christiano Buato & Mara Martinelli in the Lounge
19:00	Welcome Cocktail – Captain Gerhard Lickfett invites you for a welcome cocktail the Lounge. Suggested dinner dress: evening dress/coat and tie for the gentlemen
19:30	Captain's Welcome Dinner is served in the Dining Room
21:30	Enjoy a few requests with our pianist Robbie in the Lounge
23:00	Late Night Snack is served in the Lounge
01:30 (Friday)	ALL ABOARD SEACLOUD II prepares to put to sea
02:00 (Friday)	SEACLOUD II sails for Tallin (50 nautical miles)

Money matters: The currency in Finland is the Euro: £1 = €1.45 (approx)

Figure 10.10 An example of a ship's itinerary

Ship access

Some ships only sail in a particular area of the world and this may influence the customer's choice of cruising area. The type of ship may be the main reason for the customer's choice. The PCR and PSR will also influence the customer's selection.

The pay for working on cruise ships can be very good and it is sometimes tax free, but there is no holiday or sick pay. Most contracts include a period onboard the ship and allocated time off in a roster pattern, such as ten months on and two months off. The rosters depend on the role and seniority of the position.

Figure 10.13 Acceptable crew behaviour

- Assist passengers at the gangway and with their shopping bags when moving in and out of the tenders.

- Do not use the lifts.

- Do not sit in groups of more than three people whilst in public areas.

- Do not crowd passenger areas and remember that your place in any queue is last.

- Never be rude or short with passengers. If you are feeling low, stay out of passenger areas.

- Always wear the appropriate uniform whilst in passenger areas.

- Take your sunglasses off when talking to passengers.

- Always wear your name tag.

- No smoking or drinking alcohol whilst in passenger areas.

- Always remember to show FRIENDLY, POLITE SERVICE.

EVIDENCE ACTIVITY

P6

As a final activity, Cruise UK would like the travel agents to be aware of the different positions onboard the ship. You have been asked to create three profiles of three different jobs available within the cruise sector. These profiles should explain:

- the role and position onboard or on shore;

- the daily responsibilities;

- entry requirements;

- any special skills that are required for the job.

Special interest tourism

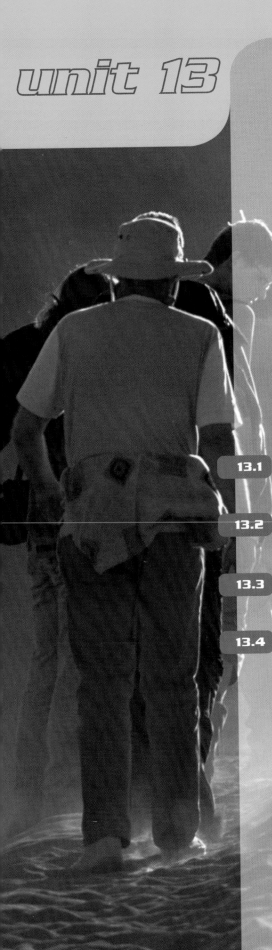

unit 13

The tourism industry is always changing and nowhere is this more evident than in the increase in the number of smaller specialist tour operators and activity organisers that have started to offer holidays. Ranging from space tourism to trekking in the Andes or outback, to canyoning along remote inland riverways, special interest tourism offers something for everybody. As people's hobbies and interests become more varied, so do the types of holidays that can be booked. The growth in the number of smaller tour operators and their focus on specific activities has led to a need for specially-trained staff. Unit 13 aims to give you an introduction to this wide industry. Jobs within specialist tour operators can often offer more variety than larger operators, and there are a number of land-based operators located overseas and in the UK who offer in-resort services to their customers.

By the end of this unit, you will:

So you want to be a...
Tour Consultant

My name Katy Simpson
Age 32
Location York
Income £18,000 plus commission

If you enjoy selling, have a keen interest in education and in building customised tours and itineraries, then this could be your job....

What do you do?

I organise and sell school educational visits.

What responsibilities do you have?

I deal with the initial enquiries from teachers, colleges and universities. Some educational institutes want a tailor-made tour that fits with a particular project. For example, a school in York twinned to one in Norway may do a joint project and want to arrange a specific visit. I find something suitable, or I design a tour specifically for them. I give the details to the group leader, sell them the tour and explain where the itinerary links with the national curriculum, the included tours and any free staff places.

How did you get the job?

I did Travel and Tourism for GCSE and then went on to the BTEC National Diploma at college. A good standard of written English is very important and so is maths, as I also have to work out the costs of the holidays and calculate free places. At my interview I had to sell one of the company's holidays from their brochure.

How did you find your current job?

It was advertised in the local paper. I sent in a CV and handwritten covering letter.

> **"** I love getting compliments from customers when I've designed a really good tour for their group **"**

What training did you get?

I shadowed an experienced tour consultant and really learnt the job that way. I also found what I'd learnt on my travel and tourism courses very useful as I already had an insight into the industry.

What are the hours like?

Usually office hours. However, we try to get in earlier than 9 a.m. on some days so that we can call teachers before they go into class.

What skills do you need?

Selling skills are very important, and listening to what the customer wants so that we match the right customer to the right product. Researching destinations and a good eye for detail are very important to get the correct itinerary.

How good is the pay?

I get a basic salary and commission on the number of tours sold. However, the commission is done on a team basis, so it is important that we all work well together.

What about the future?

I'm having a baby in 3 months time. I love the flexibility of this job, I can come back part-time. I'm not interested in moving into management, but I do enjoy training new staff. One day, I'd like to move into training sales staff.

Grading criteria

The table below shows what you need to do to gain a pass, merit or distinction in this part of the qualification. Make sure you refer back to it when you are completing work so that you can judge whether you are meeting the criteria and what you need to do to fill in gaps in your knowledge or experience.

In this unit there are 4 evidence activities that give you an opportunity to demonstrate your achievement of the grading criteria:

page 48   P1, P2, M1, M2

page 55   P3, P4, P5, M3, D1, D2

To achieve a pass grade the evidence must show that the learner is able to...	To achieve a merit grade the evidence must show that, in addition to the pass criteria, the learner is able to...	To achieve a distinction grade the evidence must show that, in addition to the pass and merit criteria, the learner is able to...
P1 Describe the development of the relationship between special interests and tourism	**M1** Explain how two relationships between special interests and tourism have developed	**D1** Assess the current market for special interest tourism, identify gaps in provision and suggest potential new products
P2 Describe three industry factors and three participant factors that affect participation in passive, active and adventure special interest tourism	**M2** Analyse how two key factors have affected participation in each of passive, active and adventure special interest tourism	**D2** Evaluate the provision for a specific special interest and justify recommendations for development.
P3 Describe the nature of activities in special interest tourism	**M3** Analyse tourism provision for a specific special interest.	
P4 Identify and show 20 key worldwide locations including passive, active and adventure activities (four should be in the UK)		
P5 Describe the tourism provision for a specific special interest, including locations and special requirements.		

13.1 *Understand the relationship between special interests and tourism*

DEFINITION

Special interest tourism is the range of tourism products based around specific products or interests. Tourists identify strongly with the location, activity, sport or hobby that is explored in greater depth during the holiday. Special interest activities can be activity-based, such as cycling or walking; based around a specific location or a past event such as Roman ruins or historic battlefields; or allow the tourist time to explore one of their existing hobbies like wine tasting or painting in greater depth, with the assistance of specialist staff and facilities. These interests may be areas in which the tourists have already participated or they may be something new that they wish to try out while on holiday. Some special interest tourism activities may be classified as 'once in a lifetime' experiences.

DEVELOPMENT OF SPECIAL INTEREST TOURISM

Mass market to special interest

When package tourism first began, the only types of holidays available as package tours to the general public were mass market holidays to seaside resorts like Spain and France. People's tastes in leisure activities have changed over time. They are more knowledgeable now about the world and have much wider leisure interests. There is a much wider choice of destinations available for holidays, and travel in general has become more common over the last 20 years. People are more adventurous and curious about the world and want to participate in many different activities, learn new skills and experience different ways of life.

The special interest market has grown to meet the change in people's lifestyles and their demand for a better service and more specialised tourist experiences. It offers tourists the chance to follow their individual interests while on holiday. Some specific factors have contributed to the growth of the specialist holiday market and these factors can be linked to the development of special interest tour operators and activity organisers.

> *Think* What types of holidays have you been on? Would you define any of them as special interest holidays?

Some of these factors include:

- Shorter working lives – people are retiring earlier and have better paid jobs, allowing for more expensive travel and for people to take more than one holiday each year.

- People now have 4 weeks paid holiday a year and there is more flexibility with regard to booking holidays.

- Due to working longer hours, people take more short breaks and often choose to pursue their leisure interests during long weekends. This has led to an increase in people booking specialist weekend breaks.

- Low-cost airlines have opened up a number of heritage and special interest resorts like Budapest and Prague. They have also increased the accessibility of many ski, lake and mountain resorts throughout Europe with low-cost flight-only options.

- Throughout the UK, people are becoming more environmentally aware and a number of tourists wish to book eco-tourism holidays or holidays which allow them to pursue environmentally-friendly activities like nature or bird watching.

- The recent increases in the number of gap years taken by young people has led to a direct increase in the number of student travel organisations offering organised gap years, round the world tickets, organised volunteer projects and sponsored expeditions.

Figure 13.1 A camel trek in an exotic location may replace the UK beach donkey ride

- Changes in the National Curriculum have led to larger numbers of schools and colleges organising educational visits both in the UK and overseas. This has led a large number of specialist tour operators who offer education tours for groups.

- A rise in the number of people who participate in sporting activities and the emphasis on healthy living has led to a corresponding rise in the number of operators offering sport-related holidays like cycling holidays. This interest in sport has also led to a number of operators offering special event holidays where participants can watch sporting events like World Cup football or rugby matches.

- The media often features adventurous destinations and holidays as articles in travel supplements. This has led to an increase in people booking specific adventure sports either as an individual activity or as a longer holiday. Unusual destinations like visiting the Titanic and space tourism have been widely publicised and are inspiring tourists to be more adventurous in their destination choice, although budget constraints may limit some tourists' wilder ideas!

- Growing awareness of the dangers of sunbathing and a greater emphasis on health have led to alternative indoor activity holidays like learning new crafts and skills and also to spa resorts becoming more popular.

- A rise in the number of single people and non-traditional families has led to more targeted holidays, which appeal to a specific market segment.

Self-actualisation

When considering special interest tourism, it is important to explore what motivates people to choose this type of holiday. People are choosing to do something just for themselves and nobody else will gain from the experience. It could be said that these people are seeking self-actualisation. They are gaining a mental rather than physical benefit from the activity.

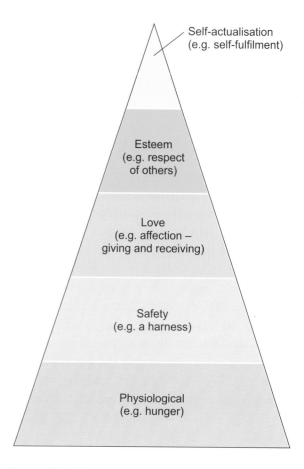

Figure 13.2 Maslow's Hierarchy of Needs

CASE STUDY: SUNSCAPE YACHTING

Sunscape Yachting is a small, independent tour operator that specialises in private yachting holidays to Turkey, Greece and Croatia.

Customers have the opportunity to sail their own yacht or to choose a traditional boat with a local crew. Customers have the choice of chartering a whole yacht or buying cabins on an exclusive boating holiday. They can also extend their holiday on land either by staying in a hotel or renting a villa. Sunscape sell land-only packages (villas, cruises and yachts) that give customers the choice of making their own travel arrangements using low-cost airlines. They also sell complete packages including flights and transfers. All customers have the services of local agents and Sunscape representatives.

Initially, the target market for these holidays appears to be rather limited as customers who charter their own yacht must be qualified by an organisation like the Royal Yachting Association. However, there are a large number of people in the UK who own yachts and are qualified skippers who might consider booking this kind of holiday. In order to expand their target market, Sunscape Yachting also offer crewed gulets, schooners and skippered yachts where customers do not need to be qualified.

While the main motivation for these holidays is relaxation, customers will also enjoy the social status that 'booking their own yacht' brings. It appeals to customers with a high disposable income (firstly because of the price and secondly because of the need for customers to be experienced sailors), therefore the target market will be the higher socio-economic groups. While a child discount is offered, this is not the kind of holiday that families with very small children are likely to book because of the safety issues with water.

As the company is not owned by any other organisation, it has to organise and pay for all principals themselves. It is unlikely that the suppliers give Sunscape very low prices,

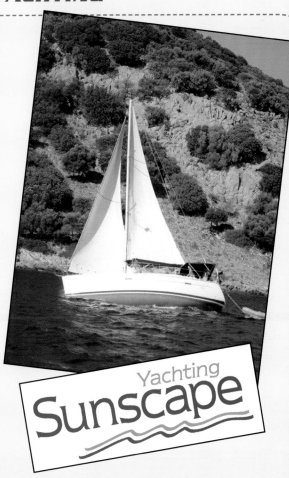

Figure 13.4 Sailing in the Mediterranean

so the prices are slightly higher than other organisations like large tour operators that offer yachting holidays. Sunscape appeals to its target market because of the exclusivity, service and the specialist knowledge of their staff. Staff knowledge will be especially important as there are many complicated additional factors to be considered, such as the costs of moorings, fuel and the rental of specialist equipment like outboard engines, windsurfers and spinnakers.

The company publishes a holiday brochure and sells its holidays indirectly to the public using travel agents, but it mainly sells directly to customers over the Internet or by telephone bookings. Run from a small office, the staff are required to undertake a range of different tasks including dealing with customer enquiries, taking bookings, and liaising with overseas staff, airlines and hotels to confirm reservations.

Crewing your own yacht would be considered to be an active special interest holiday. However, booking a holiday on a crewed yacht would be passive. These are water-based holidays with the focus of the holiday on water activities like sailing, swimming and water sports. The three countries that Sunscape currently specialises in are particularly good for yachting and water holidays. There are secluded coves that can be used for swimming and a number of small seaside villages where the yachts can moor for evening meals and overnight stops. The spectacular scenery will appeal to many customers. A number of the destinations featured, like Rhodes or Athens, also have historical and cultural attractions, which will appeal to the visiting tourists and appeal as alternative special interest attractions. The destinations are stable and exchange rates are good. Gateways are easy to access, but these destinations and holidays are seasonal and only operational during the summer.

QUESTIONS

1. What additional products do you think Sunscape Yachting could offer to its current customers?

2. If Sunscape Yachting decided to expand into another destination, where do you think that it could offer similar types of holidays?

3. If Sunscape Yachting decided to expand the products that it offered to its customers and hoped to mov e away from yachting holidays, what other special interest activities do you think the customers/existing target market might be interested in booking?

13.2 Know the factors that affect participation in special interest tourism

INDUSTRY FACTORS

Market segmentation

There is a group of special interest tour operators that do not target a specific activity, but instead appeal to a specific customer type. These include singles holidays, holidays for the over 50s, stag and hen weekends, gap year and voluntary holiday organisers. Some tour operators offer specialist accommodation to gay and lesbian couples. There are also special interest tours based around forms of transport, such as rail tours, yacht holidays and specialist cruise ships. These are all classified as special interest organisers due to their focus on a particular market segment.

Developing the attraction and appeal of events and pursuits

The range of visitor attractions that can be classed as being appealing to tourists is constantly changing and expanding. Locations which would not traditionally be considered visitor attractions like Ground Zero in New York now attract a large number of tourists. A wide number of special interest events can also be considered tourist attractions. These could involve battle or historical re-enactments, sporting events and specialist exhibitions in museums or art galleries. New activities are constantly being developed, especially in the adventure category of special interest tourism. Body surfing has only recently been offered to mainstream tourists.

As new pursuits are invented, activity organisers must try to offer them as part of their packages or tours. The visitor attractions, events and pursuits that are currently in fashion and attract tourists are highly dependent on the media and celebrities to a certain extent.

EVIDENCE ACTIVITY

P3 – P4 – P5 – M3 – D1 – D2

For P3 and P4, you must be able to describe a range of different special interest tourism activities. This should cover at least 20 separate activities, in key worldwide locations (four of which must be in the UK). Instead of just listing different activities, investigate some of the activities in depth.

A Air

- Describe three different types of air-related special interest activities.

- Name some of the providers for these named activities.

- Identify six locations around the world where these activities or other named air-based activities are offered. Two of these locations must be in the UK. Show these locations on a world map.

B Land

- Describe three different types of land-related special interest activities.

- Name some of the providers for these activities.

- Identify six locations around the world where these activities or other named land-based activities are offered. Two of these locations must be in the UK. Show these locations on a world map.

C Water

- Describe three different types of water-related special interest activities.

- Name some of the providers for these activities.

- Identify six locations around the world where these or other named water-based activities are offered. Two of these locations must be in the UK. Show these locations on a world map.

D Individual/Group

- Identify and describe two individual and two group special interest activities.

Now you have assessed the current market for special interest tourism, for D1, assess any gaps in the current market that are not currently covered by special interest tour operators.

For P5, choose one special interest that is of particular interest to you. Describe the current tourism provision for this special interest activity. You should consider:

- factors which influence tourist participation (age, health etc.);

- locations both in the UK and overseas;

- seasonality;

- climatic conditions;

- types of organisations which sell this type of holiday (independent, activity only etc.) and provision (packaged, unpackaged, ways of booking etc.);

- named examples of providers;

- tuition, instruction, levels of competence and equipment requirements for the activity.

For M3, analyse the nature of the provision, considering the different types of organisations that compete to provide this special interest activity and consider if any parts of the provision are dominant over others.

For D2, make specific recommendations on how the provision for this special interest could be improved and justify the recommendations you have made.

Roles and responsibilities of holiday representatives

Holiday representatives are the public face of tour operators and they play a pivotal role in transforming the expectations of millions of holiday-makers into reality. The work of a holiday representative can be exciting and challenging, and it is certainly varied. You will examine the roles and responsibilities of different types of holiday representatives and the legal framework in which they work to provide a safe and enjoyable holiday experience.

To be successful as a holiday representative, you will need to display a wide range of customer service skills and this unit will introduce you to the practical skills needed when dealing with holiday-makers in different situations.

By the end of this unit, you will:

14.1 Know the roles and responsibilities of different categories of holiday representatives —

14.2 Understand the legal responsibilities of a holiday representative —

14.3 Understand the importance of health and safety in relation to the role of the holiday representative —

14.4 Be able to apply social, customer service and selling skills when dealing with transfers, welcome meetings and other situations —

So you want to be a...

Holiday Representative

My name Bryony Baxter

Age 20

Income £500 per month plus commission

Live and work in a different culture, transforming holiday dreams into reality

How did you find your current job?

I completed a BTEC National Diploma in Travel and Tourism and went to Lanzarote on work experience. I shadowed holiday reps and it changed what I thought about the job. I really wanted to be a holiday rep. One of the major tour operators held a selection day at my college. I passed the selection day and was offered a job.

What are your day-to-day responsibilities?

I meet and greet any new arrivals, accompanying them on the transfer from the airport to the resort. I hold welcome meetings where we explain the various excursions that are on offer. I'm generally available to answer any questions and assist with any problems.

What are the hours like?

I get one full day off each week and usually a half day too.

What skills do you need?

It's an almost endless list. You have to be a people person and be strong enough physically to cope with very long, demanding days, and also strong emotionally to cope with complaints and sometimes abusive guests. Previous experience of customer service is essential. You need to be a reliable team player and a good communicator.

Do you need to speak a foreign language?

It's not essential, but it can help. If you're at one of the big tourist resorts, most people will speak English.

> **If you're up for a challenge, this is the job for you!**

What's the pay like?

The basic salary isn't very high, but it's paid into your UK bank account, so it's like savings really. You don't have to pay for your accommodation and you get commission on excursion sales, so it's possible to live quite well on that. We also get a free uniform, flights to the resort and discounted holidays.

What are your plans for the future?

I could become a Resort Manager or an Area Manager. Many reps go on to take up good jobs at Head Office in operations or overseas staff recruitment and training.

Grading criteria

The table below shows what you need to do to gain a pass, merit or distinction in this part of the qualification. Make sure you refer back to it when you are completing work so that you can judge whether you are meeting the criteria and what you need to do to fill in gaps in your knowledge or experience.

In this unit there are 4 evidence activities that give you an opportunity to demonstrate your achievement of the grading criteria:

page 68   P1

page 72   P2

page 76   P3, M1, D1

page 83   P4, P5, M2, M3, D2

To achieve a pass grade the evidence must show that the learner is able to...	To achieve a merit grade the evidence must show that, in addition to the pass criteria, the learner is able to...	To achieve a distinction grade the evidence must show that, in addition to the pass and merit criteria, the learner is able to...
P1 Describe the roles and responsibilities for three different categories of holiday representatives	**M1** Compare the roles and responsibilities for two categories of holiday representatives	**D1** Analyse how the roles and responsibilities of the holiday representative can contribute to the overall holiday experience
P2 Identify and explain the legal responsibilities of holiday representatives in four different holiday situations	**M2** Demonstrate effective social, customer service and selling skills when delivering a transfer speech and welcome meeting	**D2** Consistently project a confident, professional image when dealing with customers in different situations.
P3 Describe the role played by holiday representatives in creating a safe and healthy holiday environment	**M3** Deal effectively with customers in different situations and accurately complete all relevant documentation.	
P4 Use social, customer service and selling skills to deliver an arrival transfer speech and plan and deliver a welcome meeting, completing the appropriate documentation		
P5 Use social and customer service skills to deal with customers in different situations, completing the appropriate documentation.		

14.1 Know the roles and responsibilities of different categories of holiday representatives

CATEGORIES

Holiday representatives are employed by tour operators to look after the needs of holiday-makers. While representatives can also be based in the UK, the main focus of this unit is on representatives working in overseas locations.

Resort representatives have a regular presence in hotels, apartments and villas, organising excursions, offering advice and dealing with any problems that arise. Some resort representatives deal with a specific age group, such as the under 30s or the over 50s. Holiday representatives can also be found in campsites or holiday parks, and increasingly on cruise ships as a result of the considerable expansion of holidays in the cruise sector. In their busiest locations, some tour operators will also have a team of transfer representatives who are responsible for taking holiday-makers to and from their accommodation, while specialist representatives can be found working in ski resorts, in children's clubs, and as activity organisers or entertainers.

In many resorts, there is a hierarchy of team leaders, resort managers and other senior staff to provide opportunities for promotion and progression. To support their holiday representatives, many tour operators also have their own resort offices with opportunities to work as administrators.

Whatever the category, working as a holiday representative is certainly not one long holiday. No two days are the same. Each day can bring new challenges, but the work can be immensely rewarding and can provide a firm foundation for a successful career in the travel industry.

According to First Choice Holidays:

'All of our overseas positions are 100% hard work, but you'll have fun too! You'll quickly see that you'll face plenty of challenges and will need to think on your feet. But if you thrive in a fast-paced environment, you can look forward to some amazing experiences and genuine job fulfilment.'

Source: www.firstchoice4jobs.co.uk

Resort representative

The resort representative is probably the best known category of holiday representatives. They can be based in one large hotel as a property representative or be responsible for a number of properties within a resort. Some resort representatives work solely on holiday programmes for specific types of customer – for example families, the over 50s or the under 30s – while others might be allocated a specific type of accommodation, such as villas or an operator's luxury programme.

The main role of the resort representative is to look after the needs of holiday-makers in allocated properties and to transform their holiday expectations into reality. There are many duties associated with this role. It is a glamorous-sounding job, but it is actually a very demanding one with wide-ranging responsibilities.

Resort representatives are usually on hand to greet holiday-makers at their arrival airport and help with their transfer to the resort. They will have a regular presence in the properties to provide holiday-makers with information, support and additional products and services to enhance the holiday experience. In addition, resort representatives carry out behind-the-scenes activities to ensure that properties and other services are operating to the company's standards for quality and safety, and they provide an essential everyday link between the tour operator and their suppliers.

Representatives for the under 30s market

There are a number of specialist brands for young people, of which Thomas Cook's Club 18–30, MyTravel's Escapades and First Choice's 2wentys are the best known. While these representatives must carry out the standard everyday responsibilities of a resort representative, such as airport transfers, liaison with suppliers, solving problems and excursion sales, they are at the heart of the holiday activities and have an active role to play in making sure that their guests have a brilliant time. They work hard and play hard, and need to have plenty of stamina, energy and enthusiasm to work very long days, right through into the early hours of the morning.

A typical holiday for this age group has activities on the go every day, including water sports, boat cruises and even 'shop-a-thons'. By night there are live bands, night trips, clubs, top DJs and beach parties.

Figure 14.1 A team of under 30s holiday representatives

The image of the working life for this type of representative is often of one long party. However, negative publicity in recent years has led tour operators to adopt a more responsible attitude to taking young people on holiday. Organised bar crawls have been played down and the representatives have to adopt a sensible and professional approach to activities, working hard to balance the enjoyment of their guests and the sensitivities of the local population. However, problems with guests can and do still arise, often alcohol-fuelled and sometimes serious, so these representatives need to be level-headed, diplomatic and calm in a crisis.

The positions are seasonal, although tour operators offer opportunities in the winter in the UK or overseas working for other brands within their organisations. High season opportunities fit in well with higher education studies and are popular with students.

Research tip

To see some of the high-flying careers of former Club 18–30 reps, visit the website www.club18-30.com.

Representatives for the over 50s market

It is certainly not true that everyone over 50 wants a quiet holiday with nothing more exciting than afternoon tea and a game of bridge! Saga Holidays, the market leader in providing holidays for the over 50s, has always been at the forefront of developing holidays to meet the changing demands of baby boomers and the older generation. Saga offers everything from a week in Torquay to safaris and hot air ballooning in Kenya. The representatives they employ reflect the nature of their many different types of holidays.

Key words

Baby boomers – mainly people in their 50s and early 60s, born after 1946. The term relates to the high number of babies born after World War 2.

The roles and responsibilities of representatives employed for the over 50s are very much the same as those for resort representatives on standard package holidays. However, due to the age profile, many of their customers will be well-travelled people who can be quite demanding and will appreciate having a more experienced representative.

Representatives may find that they are dealing with guests into their 80s or older who might be less active and have specific needs which must be catered for. Representative positions with the over 50s operators are therefore better suited to people with broader life experiences and the ability to empathise with the needs and expectations of this age group.

Think What type of personality traits do you think are required to be an over 50s representative?

Research tip

Look at the range of holidays offered by Saga Holidays and the different categories of staff employed by the company www.saga.co.uk.

Ski representatives

The requirements for ski representatives vary from company to company. Some ski reps are based in hotels and offer a similar service to that of a resort representative in Spain, with the key differences being the weather and the scenery. The big advantage is that keen skiers and snowboarders can hit the slopes in their free time. Working in a ski resort is seasonal and provides opportunities for summer season representatives to gain year-round employment.

In addition to the typical responsibilities, ski representatives also organise lift passes, ski school and lessons, organise a varied après-ski programme and keep their guests informed of snow conditions.

Key words

Après-ski – social events or activities that take place after skiing.

Figure 14.2 Ski representatives enjoy some free time

Many ski operators also employ chalet hosts who run their own catered chalet. They plan menus, do the shopping, keep to a budget, and cook, clean and generally look after their guests, creating a home-from-home experience and providing information and advice.

CASE STUDY: NEILSON

Neilson Active Holidays have won a whole host of awards for their wintersports holidays and high levels of customer service. Neilson have been providing a special kind of activity holiday for over 25 years, with Ski & Snowboard holidays, Yatching holidays and Beachclub holidays across Europe and Canada. They've perfected the art of making everyone welcome, whatever their level of experience or favourite activities. Here's what they say about their representatives:

'As a ski representative, you will be a member of our frontline team, meeting guests on a daily basis. Your primary task will be to ensure the well-being and welfare of our guests during their stay. You will also be required to provide a ski-leading service for guests up to five days per week. Responsibilities include: accompanying airport transfers; holding weekly welcome meetings; daily hotel visits; preparing and operating a snow-focused programme of events; financial accounting; health and safety audits; completing company paperwork; general admin tasks; and ensuring that the whole resort operation runs smoothly.

The ideal candidate should be educated to GCSE standard or equivalent and have a good command of French, German or Italian. Experience of working in a customer service industry is essential. You should be a strong communicator and confident that you can work independently. All ski representatives must be physically fit, able to ski or board to an advanced level and preferably hold a skiing qualification.'

Source: www.neilson.co.uk

QUESTIONS

1. Using the company website, find out where in the world you could work as a ski representative with Neilson.

2. Find out what the opportunities are for summer work with Neilson.

Transfer representatives

Transfer representatives are employed by some of the larger tour operators in their busiest airports. Palma Airport on the island of Mallorca is a gateway for holiday destinations all over the island. Some resorts are several hours by coach transfer from the airport.

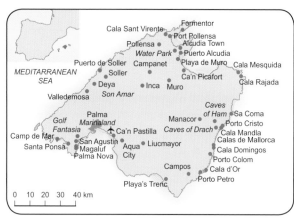

Figure 14.3 Map of Mallorca showing Palma Airport and resorts

With flights arriving from many regional airports in the UK, arrival days can be very hectic, so transfer representatives are employed in the peak summer months to help resort representatives to cope with the sheer volume of passengers. It is a very demanding job, with many potential problems to solve, including lost and damaged luggage, delayed flights, missed flights and coach breakdowns.

Transfer representatives meet and greet holiday-makers at the arrival airport, direct them to their coach, and accompany them to their resort accommodation, providing a commentary on the way. They make sure that guests are checked into their accommodation and know when and where the welcome meeting will be taking place.

On the return journey, transfer representatives pick up guests from their accommodation, check that they have got all their belongings and travel documentation, and transfer them by coach to the airport where they direct them to the correct check-in desks for their departure.

Resort safety

Resort safety issues vary, but they could include strong sea currents, systems of warning flags, busy roads (including driving on the right), muggings and staying safe in the sun.

Excursions and activities

All venues should meet required safety standards, especially in terms of fire and water safety and food hygiene, and also in terms of managing capacity and overcrowding.

MINIMISING RISKS

Prior to contracts being agreed, it is expected that tour operators have carried out health and safety audits of the properties they will be using and that the contracts would include details of minimum standards for health and safety. Some of the large tour operators employ health and safety officers in the resorts and some also use the services of experts to help them with health and safety issues, such as carrying out safety checks and risk assessments.

PROVIDING INFORMATION

During the transfer commentaries and welcome meetings, representatives are required to point out any potential risks to their guests, such as advising guests if the swimming pool is unsupervised and reminding them not to allow children to play unaccompanied in or around the pool. They must reinforce these messages on noticeboards and in their information books. Despite such warnings, the tour operator could still be held liable if anything goes wrong.

Routine procedures

Holiday representatives must take responsibility for looking out for hazards and identifying potential risks as part of their daily routine. Any new hazards must be reported immediately and actions recorded until the risk has been eliminated. This could mean closure of a facility or the withdrawal of a service that is deemed to be unsafe. If a representative is unable to resolve an issue themselves, they must ensure it is taken up by someone with authority.

Representatives must follow their company's guidelines for completing health and safety inspections and make sure that reports are filled in accurately and comprehensively. Company procedures for carrying out risk assessments must be followed. This is particularly applicable to children's representatives when introducing new activities.

Reporting incidents

It is essential that representatives submit clear, factual and accurate reports of any accidents or incidents (including outbreaks of illness), in case customers decide to take action for damages or make insurance claims. Tour operators have special report forms for this purpose.

ACCIDENT/ INCIDENT REPORT FORM

Date of accident/incident: / /
Time of accident/incident:

Exact location of accident/incident:

Weather at the time of accident/incident:

Describe the accident/incident and how it happened:

Was a photograph of the location taken?

CUSTOMER DETAILS

Customer's full name: Booking ref:

Accommodation name: Room no:

Nature of injury/illness:

Names, dates and times of any medical assistance provided:

WITNESS DETAILS

1. Name:
Relationship to customer if applicable:
Address:

2. Name:
Relationship to customer if applicable:
Address:

FORM COMPLETED BY:

Name:

Position:

Date of completion:
Signature:

Complete a sketch on the reverse of this form, if appropriate

---

Figure 14.7 An example of an accident report form

Federation of Tour Operators (FTO)

The Federation of Tour Operators (FTO) plays a key role in improving standards for the health and safety of holiday-makers on package holidays. They produce a preferred code of practice for tour operators containing 'the fundamental requirements' in a property regarding fire safety, food hygiene, pool safety, general safety, beach safety, children's clubs, villa safety, incident investigations, natural disasters and communicable diseases.

> **Research tip**
>
> To find out more about the work of the FTO, check out their website at www.fto.co.uk

EVIDENCE ACTIVITY

P3 – M1 – D1

1. There will be a number of information stands on display at the recruitment roadshows. For P3, one of your responsibilities is to prepare information sheets that describe the part played by the holiday representative in creating a safe and healthy holiday environment.

You should include a description of risks and hazards and the ways in which representatives can minimise these risks in relation to:

- accommodation;

- facilities, e.g. swimming pools, balconies, children's playgrounds, children's clubs, lifts;

- fire safety;

- hygiene;

- coach safety;

- resort safety;

- excursions and activities.

2. At the end of one of the roadshows, you are approached by someone who cannot make up their mind about whether to apply for the position of property representative or transfer representative. You deal with their enquiry and decide that it would be useful to produce some written comparisons for display at future roadshows.

For M1, select one type of property representative (hotel, youth or over 50s) plus another category (ski, children's or transfer) and produce a written comparison of the roles and responsibilities of the two jobs, highlighting similarities and differences, not just in terms of what each one does, but also including legal and health and safety responsibilities.

You have been very pleased with the roadshows and are looking forward to returning overseas to carry on with what you feel is a very worthwhile and rewarding job. You are therefore annoyed to read an article in the trade press, which suggests that holiday representatives are an unnecessary extravagance that could easily be replaced by telephone helplines in the resort.

You feel so strongly about your profession that you decide to respond with an article that analyses how the roles and responsibilities of the holiday representative contribute to the overall holiday experience. For D1, draw on everything you have completed so far to analyse the important role of holiday representatives in relation to their responsibilities to the customer, organisation and suppliers.

14.4 *Be able to apply social, customer service and selling skills when dealing with transfers, welcome meetings and other situations*

SOCIAL SKILLS

In the course of their work, holiday representatives meet people from many walks of life with differing needs, expectations and demands. Social skills are at the very heart of what they do and a good representative is able to use a range of social skills to make people feel at ease, whoever they are and whatever the situation. Social skills come naturally to some people. However, these skills can be developed with practice and by focusing on:

- providing a warm welcome, regardless of the time of day or the situation;

- creating a rapport by showing an interest in customers and making them feel at ease;

- empathising by seeing a situation from the customer's point of view;

- providing a helpful and friendly service with a smile and conversation;

- choosing the right type of language for different circumstances;

- dealing appropriately with different customers for different types of situation.

These skills need to be embedded in the representative's everyday dealings with their guests, colleagues and suppliers, whether during transfers, excursions, welcome meetings or carrying out other duties in the resort. Social skills alone don't make a good holiday representative, but when combined with customer service skills, they could make an excellent one.

CUSTOMER SERVICE SKILLS

The customer service skills described on pages 117–126 of Book 1 are applicable to holiday representatives.

Holiday representatives are judged by the standard of service they provide to the customer. This is monitored by responses given in customer service questionnaires at the end of a holiday. Tour operators whose representatives excel in customer service will have the edge over others, which in turn could increase repeat business and recommendations. It is understandable that great emphasis is placed on customer service skills.

Product knowledge

Guests expect their representatives to know everything about the resort, accommodation, excursions and the company. They must source and provide local information for their transfers and welcome meetings and support this with information books and noticeboards. Going on excursions, visiting local tourist offices, reading guidebooks and talking to the locals all help to develop knowledge of the product.

> ***Think*** What other activities could help a representative to find out more about the resort where they are working?

Identifying customer needs

Identifying and meeting customer needs is at the heart of customer service. Representatives need be able to judge a customer's body language and mood and to master the art of effective questioning and listening to help them to identify customer needs. They also need to be sensitive to customers with special needs and to offer assistance in a professional and unobtrusive way.

> **Example**
>
> Organising a room swap to a lower floor for a family with small children or organising a suitable table in the restaurant for someone using a wheelchair.

Dealing with queries

Whether a guest wants to know the long-range weather forecast, where to buy a sombrero, how to work the air conditioning in their room or how to make an insurance claim, representatives have to be prepared to respond in a positive and helpful way. A representative with good social and customer service skills tries to anticipate customer needs and make it their business to find out what they don't know to respond effectively to queries.

Providing information for different purposes

As well as providing information to guests, representatives are also responsible for making sure that special requests and room requirements have been passed to property owners and that excursion sales figures have been passed to the resort office or ground handler. If representatives are working in a team, they need to make other team members aware of any problems they have been dealing with, so that there is some continuity between the team.

Handling complaints

Booking conditions specify that complaints must be brought to the attention of the representative. This is probably the representative's least favourite part of the job, especially when they feel that the complaint isn't justified, such as not enjoying foreign food. However, sometimes things can go wrong and this results in serious and justified complaints.

Research tip

Find out some examples of different types of complaints by visiting a consumer website, such as www.holidaytruths.co.uk.

Some useful tips for handling complaints are:

- stay calm and polite;
- don't take things personally;
- don't argue;
- don't blame someone else;
- don't promise something that can't be achieved. It's better to 'under promise' and 'over deliver';
- don't accept liability;
- stay loyal to the company.

There are some simple steps to follow.

Step 1   Find out exactly what the problem is by questioning and active listening.

Step 2   Empathise and show that you understand how they feel by using positive body language.

Step 3   Confirm that your understanding of the problem is correct and take control to resolve it.

Step 4   Agree on a course of action, making sure that it meets with the customer's approval.

Step 5   Carry out what has been agreed, check on progress and report back to the customer until the problem has been resolved.

Tour operators prefer complaints to be dealt with in the resort where possible and representatives may offer 'sweeteners', such as a bottle of wine or a free excursion as a goodwill gesture.

Figure 14.8 A representative talking to guests

OTHER SITUATIONS

Sometimes non-routine incidents occur. This could mean having to deal with a guest who is distressed after being mugged or the parents of a child who has had an accident in the children's club. You may even have to deal with a death. Tour operators have procedures for dealing with different types of incidents and representatives must follow these, while looking after guests who may be upset and emotional at the same time. Sometimes, a serious incident occurs, such as a coach crash or a hotel fire, and special emergency procedures are put into place to deal with these.

It is not possible for tour operators to provide guidelines for every eventuality and representatives need to display common sense, care and attention. Most tour operators also have a 24-hour duty office in the UK where representatives can seek advice.

EVIDENCE ACTIVITY

P4 – P5 – M2 – M3 – D2

It's the end of the recruitment season and you are pleased to be back in the resort. You are now going to be helping to train the new recruits in your resort.

For P4, your first task is to demonstrate an effective arrival transfer speech. Using a microphone, welcome your guests and deliver a suitably structured arrival transfer speech. Include:

- introductions;

- safety and comfort on the coach;

- country information;

- transfer details;

- resort information;

- promotion of excursions and company services;

- procedures for accommodation check-in.

Now you must show the trainees how to organise a welcome meeting.

1. Produce invitations, a room layout plan, promotional materials and visual aids for a welcome meeting.

2. Deliver a suitably structured welcome meeting. Include:

- resort information;

- accommodation information;

- the sale of at least one excursion and one other service;

- safety information.

3. Accurately complete an excursion booking form, tickets and receipts.

You must demonstrate social, customer service and selling skills while carrying out these tasks.

For M2, you must demonstrate effective social and customer service skills in your transfer speech and welcome meeting, and use selling skills to close the sale during your welcome meeting.

For P5, as part of their induction, the trainees will have to show that they can deal effectively with a complaint and a non-routine situation involving different types of customers, as well as completing all relevant documentation. You will demonstrate how this should be done in role play situations.

You must show social skills and customer service skills when dealing with customers in at least two different situations, completing the appropriate paperwork.

For M3, demonstrate that you can deal effectively with different customers in two complex situations in tasks 1, 2 and 3 and accurately complete all relevant documentation.

For D2, demonstrate that you can consistently project a professional image when dealing with customers in different situations.

Passenger Transport Issues

Although the UK is a relatively small and heavily-populated country, both domestic and inbound tourists require an effective passenger transport network. Most inbound tourists arrive by air, which makes passenger transport vital.

In this unit, the passenger transport industry is examined, together with development, technological advances and a rise in customers' expectations. The unit also looks at how passenger transport is integrated into the rest of the industry as a vital component. The unit also looks at how the level and efficiency of particular networks can have a marked effect on the appeal and popularity of certain areas.

By the end of this unit, you will:

So you want to be a...

Passenger Transport Manager

My name Matthew Wilkins

Age 28

Location Bath

Income £33,000

What do you do?

I'm a passenger transport manager, responsible for the planning, delivery and organisation of all the public transport in the region where I work.

What does a typical day involve?

I manage the daily activities at several transport locations. That means looking at pricing, service levels, timetables and so on. I organise work rotas, deal with security alerts and complaints, meet customers face-to-face, get involved in marketing, organise passenger surveys, write reports on performance and targets, deal with the media and a host of other things.

How did you find your current job?

I was in post as the deputy when Frank, my boss, announced his retirement. He tipped me off about it and thought I would be ideal to take over. I still had to apply and go through the recruitment and selection process. It was tough, probably more for me than the other candidates.

How did you get the job?

I was working for the local council already, straight out of college with my BTEC National Diploma in Travel and Tourism. That was seven years ago now.

What training have you had?

I've done up to level 5 with the Chartered Institute of Logistics and Transport with distance learning. I paid for level 3 and the council has funded levels 4 and 5. There's been plenty of in-house training too in human resources, financial matters and other things.

What are the hours like?

It should be nine to five. Sometimes it's not unknown for me to work from six in the morning to eight in the evening. That tends to happen if there is a security alert or the weather is bad and we have to rethink the transport for the day.

What skills do you need?

You need to be an all-rounder really. A good grounding in travel and tourism is a must, but beyond that you need to be a jack-of-all-trades. Sure, you have experienced staff to help out, but at the end of the day, the decisions are down to you. You've got to think things through quickly and be decisive.

How good is the pay?

Not bad I suppose. I'm about halfway through the pay scale that creeps up to nearly £60,000.

What are your plans for the future?

I fancy moving to a big city with a really complicated transport network. London or somewhere like that would be a real challenge.

> **" If you're up for a challenge, this is the job for you! "**

Grading criteria

The table below shows what you need to do to gain a pass, merit or distinction in this part of the qualification. Make sure you refer back to it when you are completing work so that you can judge whether you are meeting the criteria and what you need to do to fill in gaps in your knowledge or experience.

In this unit there are 3 evidence activities that give you an opportunity to demonstrate your achievement of the grading criteria:

page 104   P1, M1, M1

page 109   P3, M2, D1

page 115   P4, P5, M2, D2

To achieve a pass grade the evidence must show that the learner is able to...	To achieve a merit grade the evidence must show that, in addition to the pass criteria, the learner is able to...	To achieve a distinction grade the evidence must show that, in addition to the pass and merit criteria, the learner is able to...
P1 Describe passenger transport operations within the UK	**M1** Explain how the UK passenger transport sector responds to developments and factors	**D1** Evaluate the extent to which passenger transport in the UK supports the economic growth of tourism, making reference to specific examples
P2 Describe three significant developments and three factors affecting and influencing passenger transport within the UK	**M2** Recommend and justify realistic measures to enhance relationships between passenger transport and the UK travel and tourism industry	**D2** Evaluate the contribution of passenger transport provision to the popularity and appeal in a specific tourist destination, making recommendations for improvements.
P3 Explain the relationships between UK passenger transport networks and the travel and tourism industry	**M3** Assess the effectiveness of passenger transport in a specific tourist destination and the effect on its popularity and appeal to tourists.	
P4 Describe five types of passenger transport provision in a specific UK tourist destination		
P5 Explain how passenger transport provision can influence the popularity and appeal of tourist destinations.		

15.1 *Know about passenger transport operations within the UK*

UK PASSENGER TRANSPORT PROVISION

The UK is a relatively small island, but it has the broadest possible range of passenger transport provision. For many years, passenger transport was dominated by rail. This was superseded by road transport, but the railway network is now enjoying a revived popularity due to increased investment in its infrastructure.

At the same time, a large number of regional airports have been developed across the country from Stornoway and Wick in the north of Scotland to Penzance and Plymouth in the southwest corner of England.

This section looks at the different types of passenger transport provision with a particular emphasis on their contribution to the travel and tourism industry.

Scheduled domestic flights

Until recently, there were only a handful of British airports that served the domestic market. The majority of these could be considered as international transport hubs. Over the past few years, a number of relatively small and under-used airports have been expanded. These smaller airports have contributed towards the creation of a comprehensive network, which offers both international and domestic tourists the opportunity to travel quickly and efficiently in the UK itself.

As seen in the table below, which was prepared for the Department for Transport, there has been a considerable growth in the number of passengers flying on domestic, scheduled flights. From 1998 to 2020, it is predicted that the mid-season figures will have more than doubled.

Forecast terminal passenger numbers at UK airports, 1998 to 2020 (m)

Year	International			Domestic			Total		
	Low	Mid	High	Low	Mid	High	Low	Mid	High
1998		104.1			33.6			160.2	
2005	152.8	158.5	164.4	40.7	42.2	43.8	220.5	228.8	237.4
2010	179.5	193.0	267.5	46.7	50.2	54.0	256.8	276.1	296.8
2015	211.0	224.7	261.1	53.8	59.8	66.5	299.5	333.2	370.6
2020	247.0	284.0	326.6	61.7	71.0	81.7	348.5	400.7	460.8

Note: Total figures include miscellaneous traffic category not in the international or domestic figures.

Table 15.1 Forecast terminal passengers numbers at UK airports, 1998 to 2020 predicted
Source: www.dft.gov.uk

This second set of figures prepared by the Department for Transport breaks down the forecasted passenger numbers in the domestic market itself. It is important to note that the Department for Transport has identified three distinct zones:

- London regional — domestic, scheduled flights involving at least one of the London airports, including Stansted and Luton;

- Intra-regional — effectively covers all other flights, for example, from Inverness to Leeds Bradford;

- UK Channel Islands — all flights into and out of Jersey, Guernsey and Alderney.

Forecast passenger numbers in the domestic market (millions)

Year	London Regional			Intra-regional			UK Channel Islands			Total		
	Low	Mid	High	Low	Mid	High	Low	Mid	High	Low	Mid	High
1998		22.3			9.4		33.6	1.9			33.6	
2005	26.7	27.7	28.8	11.3	11.7	12.2	42.2	2.7	2.8	40.7	42.2	43.8
2010	30.5	32.8	35.3	13.3	14.3	15.3	50.2	3.2	3.4	46.7	50.2	54.0
2015	34.9	38.8	43.2	15.6	17.3	19.3	59.8	3.7	4.0	53.7	59.8	66.5
2020	39.8	45.8	52.7	18.3	20.1	24.1	71.0	4.2	4.8	61.7	71.0	81.6

Notes: 1. Domestic passengers are counted at the airports at both ends of the journey, with the exception offlights to the Channel Islands where passengers are only counted at mainland airports.
2. 1998 figures are actuals.
3. Totals may not sum due to rounding.

Table 15.2 Forecast passenger numbers in the domestic market
Source: www.dft.gov.uk

It is valuable to look at some of the regional airports that have joined the network in recent years in order to see how they have developed.

- Blackpool (www.blackpoolinternational.com) connects to Belfast, the Isle of Man, Dublin and Stansted. Ryanair cancelled its twice-daily flights between Blackpool and Stansted in June 2007, despite the fact that it had carried over half a million passengers on the route since it was launched in 2003.

- Leeds Bradford (www.lbia.co.uk) flies to a variety of locations, including Aberdeen, Inverness, Edinburgh, Glasgow, Heathrow, Southampton, Bristol, Exeter, Newquay, Belfast, Galway and Cork. It was a considerable blow for Leeds Bradford airport when British Airways pulled out, terminating their flights to Gatwick. Nevertheless, 2006 was a record year for the airport, with almost 2.8 million passengers travelling to over 65 destinations.

- Bristol (www.bristolairport.co.uk) flies to all major Scottish airports and connects to Leeds Bradford, Manchester, the Isle of Man, Norwich and Exeter. It also has links to Jersey and Guernsey, four airports in the Republic of Ireland and Belfast. Bristol is a major centre for easyJet, Air Southwest and Flybe. British Airways dominates the business market between Bristol and Scotland.

- Norwich (www.norwichairport.co.uk) flies to three major Scottish airports, Dublin, Bristol, Exeter, Manchester and the two largest Channel Islands. Norwich is the eastern-most airport in the UK. Flybe has established itself as one of the most important airlines based here. There are considerable developments planned to improve the runway, check-in areas, shops and parking, which should lead to a slow but steady expansion.

- Exeter (www.exeter-airport.co.uk) links wih the three major Scottish airports, Belfast and Dublin. There are also flights to Manchester, Leeds Bradford, Newcastle and Norwich. Exeter also links with the two largest Channel Islands.

As Exeter is relatively close to its two major competitors, Bristol and Southampton, the airport has tended to focus on more northern domestic connections, limiting its appeal for the time being.

- Cardiff (www.cwlfly.com) flies to Glasgow, Edinburgh, Newcastle, Belfast and three cities in the Republic of Ireland. A number of different airlines have moved in since British Airways left Cardiff. Some other routes have been tested, such as Newquay and Manchester, but these have now been cancelled due to poor demand.

- Inverness (www.hial.co.uk) flies to the Orkneys and the Hebrides, three London airports, Southampton and Bristol in the southwest, two Midlands airports and a number of airports in the north, as well as Dublin and Belfast. Inverness provides a vital connecting service between the most northerly point of the British Isles and the south of England. There is a growing range of domestic flights, including those provided by Ryanair and Flybe.

> **Think** Why do you think major airlines like British Airways no longer offer flights to and from some of these smaller airports?

Research tip

For a comprehensive view of the UK scheduled domestic flight network, visit www.flightmapping.com. Select Flight Maps and then UK and Ireland from the mini world map. Hover the cursor over an airport name to reveal the current domestic flight routes. Click on the airport to go to a new page, which gives links to current news about the airport, as well as details about flights and developments.

Rail

The UK rail industry, including local, long distance, light rail and underground services, handles 2.7 million passenger trips every day. Almost 1.7 million of these are commuter trips, accounting for 63% of the total. There are 552,000 leisure journeys undertaken each day, which is 21% of the total. The vast majority of outbound leisure trips take place between 06:30 and 09:00, with return trips beginning at 16:00 and tailing off after 19:00.

The largest group of leisure users of the rail service is the 45 to 59 age group, accounting for 23% of the total. These figures are based on the Annual National Rail Travel Survey report, which bases its figures on over 400,000 questionnaires.

There is a wide variety of different train operators that provide passenger services. The Department for Transport grants them franchises. They must apply for a licence to operate from the Office of Rail Regulation.

Key words

Franchises – an agreement between one business or organisation that allows a second business to run an operation on their behalf

The key train operating companies are:

- Arriva Trains Wales (www.arrivatrainswales.co.uk)
- c2c (www.c2c-online.co.uk)
- Central (www.centraltrains.co.uk)
- Chiltern (www.chilternrailways.co.uk)
- First Great Western (www.firstgreatwestern.co.uk)
- Gatwick Express (www.gatwickexpress.co.uk)
- Great North Eastern Railways (www.gner.co.uk)
- Heathrow Express (www.heathrowexpress.com)
- Hull Trains (www.hulltrains.co.uk)
- Island Line (www.island-line.co.uk)
- Merseyrail (www.merseyrail.org)
- Midland Mainline (www.midlandmainline.com)
- Northern Rail (www.northernrail.org)
- One (www.onerailway.com)
- Stansted Express (www.stanstedexpress.com)
- First Scotrail (www.firstgroup.com)
- Silverlink (www.silverlink-trains.com)
- Southeastern Railway (www.setrains.co.uk)
- South West Trains (www.swtrains.co.uk)
- Southern (www.southernrailway.com)
- First Capital Connect (www.firstcapitalconnect.co.uk)
- Transpennine Express (www.firstgroup.com)
- Virgin Trains (www.virgintrains.co.uk)

Passenger journeys (millions)		1992/3	1993/4	1994/5	1995/6	1996/7	1997/8	1998/9	1999/00	2000/1	2001/2	2002/3
National Rail network	ZCKN	770	740	735	761	801	846	892	931	957	960	976
London Underground	KNOE	728	735	764	784	772	832	866	927	970	953	942
Docklands Light Railway	ZCKO	7	8	12	14	17	21	28	31	38	41	46
Glasgow Underground	ZCKP	14	14	15	14	14	14	15	15	14	14	13
Tyne and Wear Metro	ZCKQ	39	39	37	36	35	35	34	33	33	33	37
West Midlands Metro	ZCKR								5	5	5	5
Croydon Tramlink	GEOE									15	18	19
Manchester Metrolink	ZCKS	8	11	12	13	13	14	13	14	17	18	19
Stagecoach Supertram (Sheffield)	ZCKT			2	5		9	10	11	11	11	12
All rail	ZCKU	1,566	1,547	1,577	1,627	1,660	1,771	1,858	1,967	2,061	2,054	2,068
of which: light rail	GENZ	54	58	63	68	73	79	85	94	120	127	136

Table 15.3 Passenger journeys by rail transport
Source: Compiled using data from Railtrack, Strategic Rail Authority, Transport for London and Passenger Transport Executives and Operators

The UK railway network does not only consist of a mix of local and long distance rail services. There are established routes between the major cities and urban areas in the UK.

Research tip

To see how the National Rail network is structured visit www.nationalrail.co.uk. Click on 'Train companies and maps' and then select 'Rail maps'. On the next page, select 'National Rail network maps'.

The rail operators tend to focus on regional parts of the network, but some provide long distance connections between London and Scotland, for example. Some of the rail operators cover entire geographical areas of the UK, such as One, which covers the whole of East Anglia with connections into London.

Research tip

Using the National Rail website given above, click on the network map page and select 'National Rail passenger operators'. How many different operators are there? How many are owned by the same company?

Cities like London operate as hubs between connecting parts of the overall railway network. This means that passengers have to transfer from one train station to another in the city in order to connect to a different train, which takes them into a different region.

Example

A passenger going from Norwich to Exeter uses One, which takes them into London, terminating at London Liverpool Street. In order for them to continue their journey to Exeter, they would have to transfer across London to Victoria station, where they could pick up a South West train to their destination.

The overall National Rail network actually comprises of a mix of slow-moving local railway networks, which connect to major transport hubs, where fast inter-regional trains can be accessed. There are hundreds of small railway stations scattered across the British Isles, which are connected by a vast network of local tracks and services.

There are two more important aspects related to rail operations in the UK that are not considered to be part of the mainline train system. The first aspect relates to the two major underground railway systems. One is based in London and it is an extensive network in its own right, extending out from the centre of the city into the region inside the M25 motorway. It serves as a system for commuters, as well as an important and efficient way for domestic and overseas tourists to access parts of the capital.

The other major underground system is known as the Strathclyde Passenger Transport Glasgow Subway. This is also a major underground railway system, which carries 13.31 million passengers per year. However, it is much smaller than the London Underground, which deals with 3 million passengers every day.

Example

Figure 15.1 shows the West Yorkshire local rail network. Leeds is at the centre of the hub where most of the local rail networks pass, begin or terminate. Leeds operates as an inter-regional hub. It serves as a centre to transfer from one local line to another, as well as acting as the main station to access other larger towns and cities in the region, other destinations in the UK and as an access point to other modes of transport, including scheduled flights from Leeds Bradford airport.

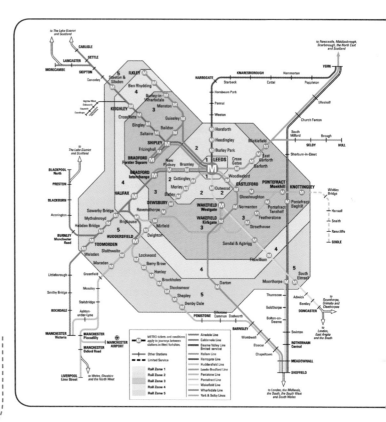

Figure 15.1 West Yorkshire local rail network

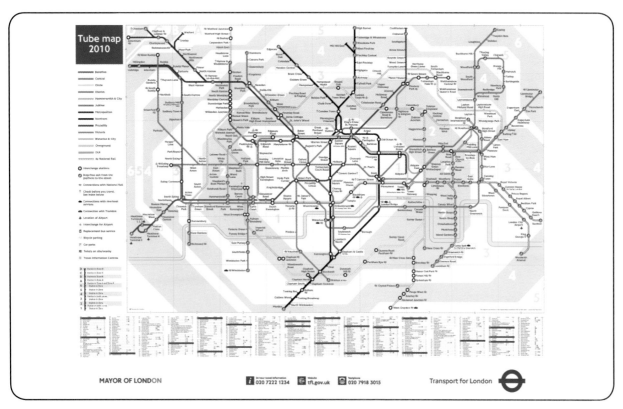

Figure 15.2 London Underground network map

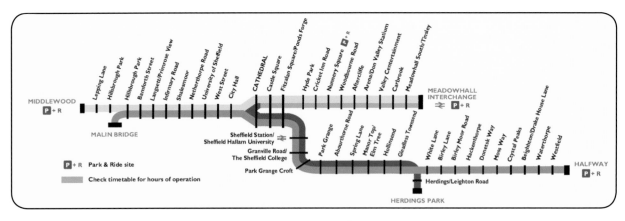

Figure 15.3 Route map for the Sheffield Supertram network

The second major addition to the overall rail provision is the light railway and tramway systems. These both use vehicles running on rails, and tramways are often partly run on roads. They both tend to be powered by overhead lines. Both systems are usually restricted to major cities. In London there is the Docklands Light Railway and the Wimbledon to Croydon tram, and in Sheffield there is the Supertram Network.

There is one final, yet significant, part of the overall rail system, but it is not actually part of the national network because of its special nature. These are often referred to as heritage railways, with a maximum speed of 25 miles per hour. These minor railways are both publicly and privately owned, depending on their source of funding. They seek to preserve old-fashioned locomotives and rolling stock, as well as outdated railway infrastructure, such as stations and narrow-gauged track. Their main aim is to replicate the look and operating practices of historic railway companies.

Example

The Talyllyn Railway celebrated its golden anniversary in 2000. It operates near Cardigan Bay in Wales. Much of its route is within the Snowdonia National Park and while it is a form of passenger transport, it is a mainly a visitor attraction as there are numerous stops along the route with visitor facilities and services.

Bus

Private operators provide around 83% of all bus services that operate outside London. The government passed the Transport Act in 2000 in order to secure a better quality of bus travel. Most buses could be considered to be scheduled services with clearly defined timetables. Local residents use them extensively, but they also provide vital linking services between various tourist attractions and major transport hubs within a particular area or region.

Figure 15.4 Many bus services are provided by private operators

Taxis and private hire

Taxis are vehicles that are licensed for immediate hiring. They can be found at taxi ranks, but they can also be hailed on the street or booked in advance. They are different from private hire vehicles, which are only licensed to collect passengers that have already booked with a licensed operator.

Both the vehicles and their drivers have to be licensed in order to make sure that they meet with minimum legal requirements. They have a maximum capacity of eight passenger seats. Local authorities will license both types of vehicle and driver. In many areas, particularly in cities, the taxis are required to be purpose-built vehicles, with a plate on the rear of the vehicle that clearly shows the taxi licence number. It is often the case that private hire vehicles are also required to have special disks on their windscreens and rear window disks to indicate their licence status.

Both types of vehicle provide a valuable service. Domestic and overseas tourists can use these vehicles to transport them to and from attractions and accommodation. Generally speaking, this type of transport tends to be used for shorter journeys only as their cost per mile is considerably higher than most other forms of transport.

Research tip

Use a search engine to find a full description of the services provided by licensed London cabs. Note that they can provide tours, day trips, airport and port transfers and guided tours of London.

Domestic ferries

The UK is an island, but there are several hundred inhabited, smaller islands around the mainland, including the Channel Islands in the southwest and the Shetlands to the north of the Scottish mainland.

Domestic ferries are services that run within the territorial waters of the UK, connecting the mainland with these islands and which do not involve transport through waters belonging to an overseas country. Domestic ferry services do not include cross-channel services to France or ferry services across the North Sea to Scandinavia. Technically, a domestic ferry service is still counted as such if it is transporting passengers from the UK mainland to Northern Ireland, but not if the ferry connects with the Republic of Ireland.

Example

The Isle of Wight lies to the south of the ports of Southampton and Portsmouth on the south coast of England. There are a number of scheduled domestic ferry services connecting four Isle of Wight ports with three UK mainland ports.

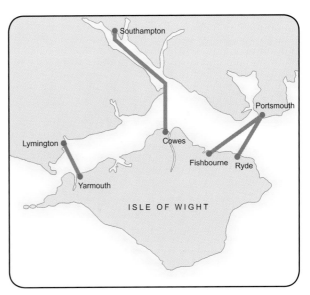

Figure 15.5 Domestic ferry connections from the UK mainland to the Isle of Wight

The Isle of Wight is a major tourist destination for domestic and overseas tourists. The island is famous for its extensive beaches and countryside.

Research tip

For further information about the Isle of Wight, visit www.iwight.com and www.wightlink.co.uk.

Scheduled coach

As part of the overall bus service, it is important to remember that there are long distance express coach services, which offer a viable alternative to rail travel as they are often more competitively priced. For journeys between 75 and 350 miles long, the market share between coaches and railways is broadly similar.

The leisure and holiday market dominates coach travel. Around 60% of all coach travel in the UK consists of organised coach tours and holiday journeys. There are some commuter coaches that go into London, such as the coach service that runs every 10 to 20 minutes between Oxford and London.

Research tip

A useful website to start research about UK coach provision is www.infotransport.co.uk. Choose the Coach travel option from the menu. For information on coach operators serving from Victoria coach station, visit www.tfl.gov.uk. Select Getting around, and then choose Victoria Coach Station.

River bus

Many major UK cities are situated along rivers. In the past, these rivers were of vital importance as far as commercial traffic and trade were concerned. River transport has been in decline for many years, but several cities have now recognised the value of river bus services as another means of moving passengers around the city and viewing the various attractions from a totally different perspective.

London is among the cities to have embraced the concept of the river bus, with numerous leisure services running on a daily basis from the early hours of the morning for commuter passengers through to early evening. There are a number of specific leisure services, which run from the centre of London, enabling tourists to visit major London attractions outside the city centre, such as Greenwich and Hampton Court. As an additional service for overseas passengers, many of the trips offer multilingual commentaries.

Example

The Hamble River Bus service runs during the main tourist season from June to September each year, connecting Hamble-Le-Rice with the Manor Farm Country Park, using the River Hamble in Hampshire. Run by Blue Star Boats, this regular service runs every 1½ hours and links a number of countryside attractions.

Figure 15.6 Many famous London landmarks can be seen from the River Thames

Other providers

The first major alternative providers are the park and ride services. These have become increasingly common on the outskirts of city centres and major towns to provide an alternative service for visitors. This avoids the visitors having to drive into the town centre and find parking. There is a wide variety of different park and ride operators providing services from Aberdeen to York and from Barnsley to Worcester.

Bus and minibus services run on a regular basis from the park and ride car parks, which are situated on the outskirts of the town or city. They operate in a similar way to the park and ride facilities provided by airports, although they are usually run by independent operators. Some of the park and ride schemes are run or subsidised by city or county councils as part of their overall strategy to reduce congestion in major urban areas.

Airports need to provide passenger transport facilities within the airport perimeter itself and also to and from parking facilities outside the airport grounds. Large airports need to provide free coach, light rail or bus services between the terminals and the main airport building. These services need to run on a 24-hour basis, ferrying passengers from their aircraft through to customs, passport control and baggage reclaim.

Passenger parking at nearly all airports is a considerable problem and there is often insufficient parking available at peak times. As a result, many subsidiary services that are usually run by private operators offer connecting bus and coach services, either from hotels or from dedicated secure parking areas. These services run on a 24-hour basis and passengers are usually charged an additional premium for the transport in addition to any payment that may have been made for the parking itself.

Research tip

For a comprehensive website on park and ride systems, visit www.parkandride.net.

1) Heathrow – 67.5m	
2) Gatwick – 34.1m	
3) Stansted – 23.6m	
4) Manchester – 22.4m	
5) Luton – 9.4m	
6) Birmingham – 9.1m	
7) Glasgow – 8.8m	
8) Edinburgh – 8.6m	
9) Bristol – 5.7m – actual figure is 5,757,963	
10) Newcastle – 5.4m	

Table 15.4 The UK's busiest airports: number of passengers
Source: CAA 2006 figures

1) Heathrow – 472,533	
2) Gatwick – 256,102	
3) Stansted – 191,876	
4) Manchester – 213,114	
5) Edinburgh – 118,690 .	
6) Birmingham – 109,194	
7) Glasgow – 99,157	
8) Luton – 83,207	
9) London City – 73,814	
10) Bristol – 65,939	

Table 15.5 The UK's busiest airports: air transport movements
Source: CAA 2006 figures

Network Rail runs, maintains and develops the UK's tracks, signalling systems, tunnels, level crossings, viaducts, bridges and 17 railway stations. They are structured around eight major routes:

- Scotland
- the northeast
- the northwest
- the west
- Anglia
- Wessex
- Sussex
- Kent

Its main purpose is to support the rail infrastructure, allowing franchised operators to safely use the tracks and facilities. On average, they upgrade 700 miles of rail each year. Network Rail only came into existence in October 2002, taking over responsibility from the privately-owned Railtrack.

FEATURES OF TRANSPORT

Each specific part of passenger transport provision has its own set of features. Some of these features are preconceived ideas from experience of these types of transport in the past, or current trends in understanding that type of transport.

As standard transport provision differs from region to region, it is difficult to make any broad generalisations about its features. Table 15.5 identifies some observations about different types of transport.

Table 15.6 The major features of different types of transport

FEATURES	AIR	RAIL	BUS	TAXI	FERRY	COACHES
Cost	Falling costs on many scheduled flights. Now no longer the most expensive option.	Relatively expensive during peak hours, although there is a wide variety of discounts and special offers available.	Relatively low cost compared to other options.	High cost per mile.	Relatively low cost.	Relatively low cost compared to other options.
Level of service	Regular scheduled flights, often several times each day.	Considerably improved and more reliable and frequent. Operators have synchronised services.	High in urban areas with frequent services. Patchy or non-existent in rural areas.	High in urban areas, low in rural areas.	Limited.	Regular scheduled services, often several times per day.
Classes available	Usually economy and business class only.	Usually first class and standard class.	Single, standard class.	Single fare structure.	Berths not usually necessary so one class as standard.	Single class structure.
Facilities provided	Flights usually too short for meals. Refreshments available. Terminals provide full range of services.	Few services on local rail networks, but enhanced services on longer distance rail journeys.	None	None	Largest physical transport – full range of facilities available.	Basic, may include refreshment and entertainment.
Accessibility	Growth of regional airports has improved accessibility. Facilities available for disabled. Multilingual signage as standard.	Access to major rail transport hubs via local stations. Some issues concerning disabled access. Fewer multilingual services than some other transport options. .	Relatively poor, unless bus is specially adapted.	Most can cope with disabled passengers.	Requires transportation to and from port or harbour. Access for the disabled is good.	Reasonable for disabled passengers. Access improved by including a number of pick-up and drop off points.
Comfort and convenience	Access to terminals less of an issue due to growth of regional airports. Most flights timed to coincide with international arrivals and departures.	Considerable investment made to improve rolling stock. Timetables organised to facilitate passenger transfer from one region to another or from one operator to another.	Acceptable for short journeys, but less so for longer journeys.	Comfort acceptable for short journeys. Convenient pick-up and drop off points.	Usually good and often only option to smaller outlying islands.	Compares well with other options. However, very reliant on road network and vulnerable to traffic delays.

> **Think** How are levels of service and issues such as value for money monitored?

Each different type of transport has its own peculiarities and differing levels of customer expectation. How are these expectations addressed?

TRANSPORT OPERATORS

There have been considerable changes in the nature of the ownership of passenger transport in the UK recently. For many years, much of the rail and bus networks were publicly owned, as were elements of the air network, such as British Airways. The overall transport network in the UK is now a mixture of private, public and non-profit sectors.

Private sector

The vast majority of transport provision is provided by the private sector. This means that the transportation is owned and run by limited companies. Many of the services used to be in the public sector, but many parts of the transport network were sold to private businesses during the 1980s and early 1990s. This process was known as privatisation and deregulation.

> **Key words**
>
> Deregulation — reducing the amount of government involvement to encourage a free market. This means removing many restrictions and regulations that previously controlled the market.

All airlines and rail companies are now privately owned. However, there is still some public involvement in the ownership of certain airport terminals, infrastructure (such as Network Rail) and part-ownership (such as the London Underground).

Most bus companies have also been privatised and deregulated. Taxi and private hire companies are privately owned, as are the domestic ferry network, scheduled coach services and the majority of river buses.

Public sector

There are elements of the transport network that are still publicly owned. These tend to be in areas where local councils or central government have made specific investments to improve the transport infrastructure. They also exist where private businesses do not consider it to be economically viable to be able to run the service and generate a profit. This means that there are still elements, such as bus and tram services, which remain within the public sector. They are heavily subsidised and considered to be necessary in order to maintain transport in a particular area.

CASE STUDY: PROBLEMS WITH BUS DEREGULATION

From 2000 to 2005, the number of passengers using buses has dropped by 7% nationally. However, at the same time it had risen by 32% in London. There have been many calls for concessionary fares to be re-introduced, not only to encourage commuters, but also tourists to consider using the bus rather than other forms of transport. Even the House of Commons recognises that many people have a poor image of buses and that there needs to be a significant overhaul in the system. The industry itself was privatised in 1985 and the government has set targets to substantially increase bus usage by 2010. Nationally, this seems to be in danger of failing. For many rural areas, bus services are a vital lifeline between small villages, market towns and services required by the local inhabitants. They could also provide a useful alternative for tourists by opening up access to more remote and under-used visitor attractions.

QUESTIONS

1. What was the purpose and reasoning behind the privatisation of the bus industry?

2. What do you understand by the term 'concessionary fare' and how could this be used to benefit domestic and overseas tourists?

3. What is meant by the term 'under-used visitor attraction'?

Non-profit sector

Non-profit passenger transport provision is relatively limited in the travel and tourism industry. The provision is mainly focused on heritage transport, which seeks to be self-financing, with the option of producing a modest profit. This can be reinvested into improvements in the infrastructure and the overall range of services offered.

The large numbers of heritage railways, which are scattered around the UK, are charity-based non-profit organisations. They rely on generating sufficient funds from their existing services in order to continue running the services and to make investments in continued conservation.

REGULATORY ORGANISATIONS

Regulatory organisations control, restrict and impose minimum standards on transport provision, regardless of the ownership or nature of the operators. A number of different organisations have been created, which are a mixture of:

- government departments, which are an integral function of central government;

- government agencies, which are semi-independent, but funded by the government and act on their behalf;

- regulatory bodies, which are usually trade associations that seek to self-govern a particular part of the industry to avoid unnecessary government intervention;

- other bodies, such as pressure groups and consumer organisations, as well as groups in the industry itself.

Government departments

The primary responsibility for passenger transport operations rests with the Department for Transport. It is responsible for ensuring that the transport system meets the needs of the economy, environment and society. The responsibility extends across the entire transport sector and it implements the government's transport strategy. The Department for Transport produces a number of strategic plans, annual reports and regulations in order to control and shape the transport system as a whole.

The department has seven executive agencies:

- The Driving Standards Agency

- The Driver and Vehicle Licensing Agency

- The Vehicle Certification Agency

- The Vehicle and Operator Services Agency

- The Highways Agency

- The Maritime and Coastguard Agency

- The Government Car and Despatch Agency

The department also sponsors nine non-departmental bodies:

- British Transport Police Authority

- Railway Heritage Committee

- Northern Lighthouse Board

- Trinity House Lighthouse Service

- Passenger Focus

- Commission for Integrated Transport

- Disabled Persons Transport Advisory Committee

- Standing Advisory Committee on Trunk Road Assessment

- Traffic Commissioners and Deputies

Government agencies

An agency is a department with special responsibility for oversight and administration of a particular part of transport operations or passenger transport.

CASE STUDY: THE DRIVING STANDARDS AGENCY

The Driving Standards Agency is a trading fund with a turnover of around £145 million in 2005/06. The income for the same year was approximately £160 million, funded by fee income and revenue from non-statutory activities. The DSA employs 2,541 staff, of which some 1,889 are driving examiners. In 2005/06, the Agency conducted over 1.9 million practical tests for car drivers, 113,000 vocational tests and over 87,000 motorcycle rider tests. Over 1.5 million theory tests were carried out at 158 centres. At the end of the year, there were 39,000 people on the Register of Approved Driving Instructors.

The DSA's mission is to contribute to the public objective to achieve a 40% reduction in riders and drivers killed or seriously injured in road accidents in the age group up to 24 years, by 2010, compared with the average for 1994 to 1998, by:

- setting standards for drivers, riders and instructors;

- driver education and the provision of learning resources;

- registering and supervising quality assured instructors;

- modern, effective and efficient assessments conducted as computer-based and practical tests.

The DSA monitors these aims through six specific outcomes:

- Delivery of effective services to customers

- Improvements in road safety

- Reduction of congestion on the roads

- Better use of regulatory powers

- Reduction of environmental damage, crime and anti-social behaviour

- Better value for money

Source: www.dsa.gov.uk

Traffic Commissioners are appointed by the Secretary of State for Transport and are responsible for the licensing of the operators of Heavy Goods Vehicles (HGVs) and buses and coaches (Public Service Vehicles or PSVs), the registration of local bus services and granting vocational licences and taking action against drivers of HGVs and PSVs.

The Traffic Commissioner for Scotland is also responsible for dealing with appeals against decisions by Scottish local authorities regarding taxi fares and appeals against charging and removing improperly parked vehicles in Edinburgh and Glasgow.

Commissioners are independent in their licensing functions. When necessary, they hold Public Inquiries, in particular to consider the environmental suitability of HGV operating centres and the possibility of disciplinary action against operators who have not observed the conditions of their licences.

The Senior Traffic Commissioner has the role of encouraging consistency in licensing decisions and procedures. Traffic Commissioners are assisted by Deputy Traffic Commissioners, who hold some of the Public Inquiries.

Regulatory bodies

A regulatory body is an organisation that has been appointed by the government to set minimum national standards and to ensure that transport operators comply with them.

Example

The Civil Aviation Authority was created in 1972 and it is the primary regulator of aviation for the UK. It has a number of responsibilities, including:

- the licensing of airports and aviation facilities;
- the licensing of aircraft;
- overseeing the Air Travel Organisers' Licensing (ATOL), which provides financial protection for those booking package holidays.

Research tip

To find out more about the work of the Civil Aviation Authority, visit their website at www.caa.co.uk.

Example

The Office of Rail Regulation (ORR) was created in 2004. Its key responsibilities are:

- to ensure that Network Rail manages the network efficiently, meeting the needs of its users;
- to encourage continuous improvements in health and safety and compliance (as well as taking enforcement action if needed);
- to license operators of railway assets, setting the terms for access to the network and other facilities.

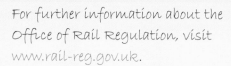

Research tip

For further information about the Office of Rail Regulation, visit www.rail-reg.gov.uk.

There is no national regulatory body for ferries to control and enforce performance and safety standards, although ferry operators are accountable to the Maritime and Coastguard Agency for safety and operational matters. There are no proposals at this time for a national ferry regulator to be created, although the Scottish parliament is considering such a move.

Other bodies

The Confederation of Passenger Transport is recognised by the government as being the primary organisation that speaks for the coach, bus and light rail industries. It negotiates on behalf of the industries with local and national government and consults the industries.

Example

Dial-a-Cab is the largest supplier of licensed taxis in central London and has a fleet of 2,200 drivers. It is recognised as being a market leader and a major voice in the taxi industry and is involved in direct negotiations with the Department for Transport.

Many other groups can be considered as pressure groups, passenger groups or lobby groups. These include:

- the RAC Foundation, which is an independent charity that was established to promote issues relating to the use of vehicles;

- Transport 2000, which is an independent national organisation concerned with sustainable transport;

- Friends of the Earth, which is concerned with the building of new roads and airports and supports alternatives to these two forms of transport, such as rail;

- Bus Users UK, which is an independent group with the aim of giving bus passengers a voice;

- Travelwatch, which is an independent organisation that seeks to be the voice of London's transport users;

- the Association of Community Rail Partnerships, which is a federation of 60 rail partnerships and rail promotion groups.

Other organisations with an indirect interest in passenger transport issues include the Countryside Alliance, the Community Transport Association, Sustrans and Railfuture, an independent organisation campaigning for better services on the rail network.

ROLE OF REGULATORS

As laid down by the government department that originally established them, the role of regulators is to ensure the following:

- The maintenance of health and safety — to ensure that passenger transport provision in the area of responsibility complies to current health and safety legislation and, if possible, exceeds the expectations of those laws.

- Ensuring compliance with the law — these can be industry-specific rules and regulations or general laws, which apply to any road, air or sea transport user.

- Improving transport infrastructure — to fund or encourage transport operators and other organisations, including councils, to invest in and consider improvements in the transport infrastructure, either in a local area or as part of the overall network.

- Improving service standards — to ensure that service levels attain set minimum levels and, if possible, to exceed these standards and to negotiate by increasing levels of service and provision with a view to a constant series of improvements over a number of years.

Think How can regulatory bodies ensure that people working in a particular industry apply the minimum standards and requirements of the regulatory body? What measures could be taken against the operators if they fail to do so?

15.2 *Understand the developments and factors affecting and influencing passenger transport in the UK*

DEVELOPMENTS

At any given time, there are new developments and trends that will have a direct influence on passenger transport provision in the UK. The priority and emphasis of each of these developments changes over time, particularly if they are brought forward in the overall debate by the government, a political party, a transport industry or a pressure group.

Here we look at four different developments that were prominent in 2007.

Toll roads

It has been estimated that sheer volume of traffic causes around 65% of congestion and it is believed that traffic will grow by over 30% over the next 5 years. Apart from congestion charges, the alternative is to consider motorway toll roads.

The first motorway toll road in the UK was opened in December 2003 in the West Midlands. The area was selected as the original M6 was designed to carry 72,000 vehicles per day, but it actually had to cope with 160,000. This meant that the average speed between Junctions 4 and 11 of the M6 dropped to 17 miles per hour.

The new M6 toll road was built to relieve one of the most congested sections of motorway in Europe. It is officially named as the M6T and was privately financed. It consists of a three-lane motorway that bypasses the busiest section of the M6 through Birmingham. It is 27 miles in length, has 8 entry and exit junctions and 6 toll stations. Drivers have to pay to use the toll road. It has been estimated that using the toll road can reduce journey times by up to 45 minutes. The M6T has been seen as a success, but it is being closely examined to see if the concept of toll roads should be rolled out to a wider network.

Congestion charging

London is an example of a major city that charges road users who access a particular part of the city. This is a very different charging system to the M6T or paying a toll to cross the river Severn or the Thames at Dartford.

It is a camera-based system that captures a car's registration plate when entering the chargeable zone. Car users are required to pay a congestion charge either in advance or on the day of travel. They can also pay a slightly higher charge the following day, but if the charge remains unpaid after that time, a penalty charge notice of £100 is sent to the registered owner of the vehicle. The congestion charge area in London has recently been expanded as a result of a number of key objectives being met. Congestion inside the zone has been reduced by 30% and traffic levels have been reduced by 18%. On any given day, there are 65,000 fewer car movements. Buses have enjoyed a surge in popularity, with 29,000 more customers each day.

High-speed rail

It is believed that the utmost capacity on the rail network, particularly between main cities, will have been reached by 2015. As a result, the Department for Business, Enterprise and Regulatory Reform and a number of other organisations are encouraging the concept of high-speed lines, which could provide up to 220 trains more per day, increasing seating capacity between cities by 50%. High-speed rail would offer high passenger capacity, which is actually 50% more than a three-lane motorway. High-speed rail would allow the journey from London to Glasgow to be undertaken in just three hours. Leeds could be reached from London in an hour and a half and Newcastle in two hours. However, the costs of high-speed lines are high and are considered by many not to be an affordable option. This is despite the fact that countries such as France and Japan have constructed a number of highly effective links.

Aircraft technology

One of the most important developments in aircraft technology has been the creation of the Airbus A380 (Figure 15.7). It compares extremely favourably in terms of seating, speed and range with the commonly used Boeing 747. Eleven passenger airlines have currently agreed to buy the new aircraft, committing to $40 billion worth of spending.

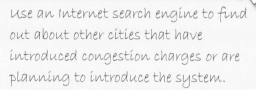

EVIDENCE ACTIVITY

P3 – M2 – D1

The Department for Culture, Media and Sport has seen your preliminary work on passenger transport operations and is interested in seeing how the passenger transport sector works in the travel and tourism industry as a whole. As an extension of your work, you have been asked to prepare the following information as part of an additional report:

- identify and explain the current relationships between the passenger transport sector and the travel and tourism industry as a whole (P3);

- explain why these relationships exist (P3).

The department is keen to identify how any existing relationships can be improved in order to enhance the travel and tourism industry as a whole. You have been asked to consider the following as part of your report:

- a recommendation of realistic measures that could enhance the relationship between passenger transport and the travel and tourism industry (M2);

- how these suggestions or recommendations would actually work in practice (M2).

The department recognises that the passenger transport industry has an important part to play in the economic success and growth of tourism. You are asked to identify and evaluate the following:

- how current provision, operation and regulation of transport operations make a positive contribution to the travel and tourism industry (D1);

- how current provision, operation and regulation of transport operations have a negative impact on the travel and tourism industry (D1).

15.4 *Understand how passenger transport provision affects the popularity and appeal of a specific UK tourist destination*

In this final section of the unit, you are required to look at a specific UK tourist destination. It is therefore difficult to give any specific advice as each tourist destination has its own unique details in terms of provision, popularity and appeal. The nature of the tourist destination itself may be radically different and rely more or less on transport provision in order to be a success.

In order to address your choices of an ideal UK tourist destination to form the basis of your study, we must first look at the different options in terms of tourist destination before looking at transport provision, popularity and appeal. We have selected Great Yarmouth as our tourist destination throughout this unit and there are a number of worked examples as indicators.

TOURIST DESTINATION

Your first major consideration is to choose a tourist destination. Ideally, this should be a compact, clearly definable area rather than one part of a major urban sprawl or specific part of a bigger region that does not have defined areas. Essentially, your choices are:

* capital cities — London, Cardiff, Edinburgh or Belfast;

* coastal resorts — it is important to choose specific resorts, such as Brighton, Hastings, Blackpool, Whitby or Southend-on-Sea, as opposed to the south coast of England or the English Riviera;

* cultural or historic towns and cities — this encompasses all other tourist destinations that do not automatically fall into the first two categories. You should choose York rather than Yorkshire or Lancaster rather than Lancashire. However, you should also investigate the whole of the town or city rather than an aspect or part of that town or city.

Great Yarmouth in Norfolk is situated with the river Yare to the west and the North Sea to the east. It is one of the UK's most popular seaside destinations with over 15 miles of sandy beaches. The Victorians helped to develop the resort as the new fashion for sunbathing transformed the focus of the resort from the town and the riverside to the beach. The oldest parts of Great Yarmouth still survive around the South Quay area.

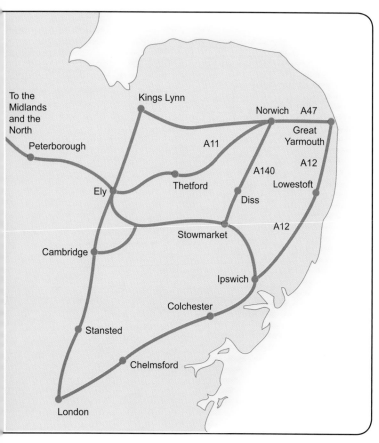

Figure 15.8 Map of Great Yarmouth area

EVIDENCE ACTIVITY

P4 – P5 – M2 – D2

Both the Department for Transport and the Department for Culture, Media and Sport recognise the value of the reports that you have created. However, both departments feel that in order to get many of the key points across, particularly in relation to the way in which passenger transport provision has a direct impact on the popularity and appeal of particular destinations, an additional study is needed. You have been asked to research and produce a study using the following guidelines:

- Select a specific UK tourist destination. (It should have a minimum of five different types of passenger transport available.) (P4)

- The area should have tourist appeal and popularity, but must be a clearly defined area. (P4)

- You should describe the current provision of transport and identify whether the destination would benefit from alternative or additional transport provision. (P4)

- Explain how passenger transport provision influences the popularity and appeal of the destination. (P5)

- Explain in more general terms how the level and quality of passenger transport provision has an impact on the popularity and appeal of tourist destinations. (P5)

As an extension of the last two parts, the departments would like you to include the following:

- An assessment of the effectiveness of the passenger transport provision to your chosen tourist destination. (M3)

- How current passenger transport provision to the area has created or sustained popularity and appeal to tourists. (M3)

- An evaluation of the contribution that current passenger transport provision has made to the specific tourist destination. (D2)

- A series of recommendations for improvements to passenger transport provision that would have a positive impact on the popularity and appeal of the area to tourists. (D2)

The Appeal and Importance of UK Visitor Attractions

Visitor attractions have been popular in the UK for far longer than many people think. Thousands of attractions have been developed over the decades and are extremely popular with domestic and inbound tourists.

This unit looks at why so many visitors are attracted to these sites and the importance of the attractions as far as local economies are concerned.

Attractions are a major part of the travel and tourism industry, ranging from natural environments and man-made structures to areas associated with art and literature. This unit gives you the opportunity to look at specific attractions, what they offer and how they operate. The unit looks at the typical types of visitors and their expectations, as well as how the attractions adapt over time to maintain and increase their appeal.

By the end of this unit, you will:

18.1 Know the products and services provided by different types of visitor attraction — page 119

18.2 Know the range and purpose of techniques used for visitor interpretation — page 124

18.3 Understand the appeal of visitor attractions to different types of visitor — page 129

18.4 Understand the importance of visitor attractions to the popularity and appeal of UK tourist destinations — page 136

So you want to be a...

Visitor Services Manager

My name Nicky Weller
Age 25
Income £20,000

If you enjoy using your language skills, meeting new people and a variety of daily challenges, then this could be for you...

So, what do you do?

I'm the Visitor Services Manager for a resort town. I'm basically desk-based – admin, telephone calls, working with staff, attractions and hotels.

What does a typical day involve?

It depends. I work closely with the suppliers of out brochures and leaflets, and with the people who do our mail shots. I do around two hours of admin and phone calls a day. I spend time with the call centre staff, and then here's often a civic function or exhibition to attend or plan for.

How did you find your current job?

I did French and German at night school while I was doing my BTEC National in Travel and Tourism. After that, I went straight into a Tourist Information Centre – a TIC – as an assistant. The council were recruiting for the season, but they offered me the full-time job when the contract finished. I was promoted to a TIC Deputy Manager within a year and ran my own TIC. About six months ago, I was promoted to my current job.

What training have you had?

When I got the deputy manager job, the council sent me on an NVQ level 4 management course. The council is really good about offering that sort of opportunity. We also get updates on IT and language refresher courses.

What are the hours like?

I'd be stressed with overload if I stuck to 9 to 5! I usually put in an hour or so after the main office has closed for the day. If I work in the evenings, say attending a function, I take the following morning off.

> ❝ **I'm looking to become Head of Tourism in a couple of years' time.** ❞

What skills do you need?

Customer care, management, IT, secretarial and language skills are all handy. Management means managing budgets, recruiting and developing staff and organising staff rotas.

How good is the pay?

I guess the ceiling here is around £30,000. I'm looking to become Head of Tourism for the resort, which will be around £40,000.

What's the likelihood of that happening?

I probably don't have enough experience at the moment, but when the current Head retires...well, I'll apply and see what happens.

Grading criteria

The table below shows what you need to do to gain a pass, merit or distinction in this part of the qualification. Make sure you refer back to it when you are completing work so that you can judge whether you are meeting the criteria and what you need to do to fill in gaps in your knowledge or experience.

In this unit there are 3 evidence activities that give you an opportunity to demonstrate your achievement of the grading criteria:

page 128   P1, P2, M1, D1

page 135   P3, M2

page 142   P4, M3, D2

To achieve a pass grade the evidence must show that the learner is able to...	To achieve a merit grade the evidence must show that, in addition to the pass criteria, the learner is able to...	To achieve a distinction grade the evidence must show that, in addition to the pass and merit criteria, the learner is able to...
P1 Describe the products and services provided by one built and one natural visitor attraction	**M1** Analyse how effectively the products, services and interpretation techniques of a built and a natural attraction are used to meet the needs of three different types of visitors	**D1** Make realistic and justified recommendations for improvements to the products, services and interpretation techniques used by a selected built or natural attraction to meet the needs of different types of visitors
P2 Describe the techniques used for visitor interpretation at one built and one natural visitor attraction	**M2** Explain how one built or natural attraction could adapt to appeal to a wider range of visitor types	**D2** Evaluate the success of visitor attractions to the popularity and appeal of a destination or area, making recommendations for improvement.
P3 Explain the appeal of one selected natural and one built visitor attraction to different types of visitors	**M3** Explain the impact visitor attractions have had on the popularity and appeal of a destination or area.	
P4 Explain why visitor attractions are important to UK tourism.		

INTERPRETATION TECHNIQUE	DESCRIPTION AND USE
Curators	A curator is an individual who cares for an attraction's collection. They are directly involved in preservation, conservation, cataloguing and interpretation. They are considered to be experts in their field and may readily take the role of guides around the attraction. They may also be used in a more formal manner, such as presenting talks on particular aspects of the collection or the attraction in a small theatre or auditorium.
Range of activities	The overall range of interpretation techniques used by an attraction is designed to contribute to the overall experience of visitors. It is likely that more sophisticated attractions will use the widest possible variety of interpretation techniques. A museum, for example, could use static displays, actors, interactive technology and the opportunity to ride, touch, feel or smell particular exhibits.
Signage	Signage not only plays a vital role in terms of orientating the visitor and pinpointing precisely where they are in the attraction, but it also is a major part of interpretation. Signage assists visitors in planning their route around the attraction, allowing them to focus on areas of the attraction that are of particular interest or are directly related to one another.

Example

The site of the 1066 Battle of Hastings in East Sussex lies below Battle Abbey. English Heritage recently made a £2.6 million investment in the creation of a major interactive exhibition. Visitors can try on chain mail and watch a computer-generated recreation of the battle in a purpose-built 40-seat auditorium. The new visitor experience, The Battle for England, uses the latest interpretation techniques and technology.

Figure 18.4 Interactive tourism experience at Battle Abbey

PURPOSE

It is rare to find a visitor attraction that has a single overall purpose that directly relates to the interpretation techniques that they have chosen. Most attractions have multiple purposes in designing their interpretation techniques. It is important to remember that all attractions will try to accommodate the needs of the widest possible range of visitors and the interpretation techniques will therefore need to be multi-purpose. The first two major purposes are interrelated as these are directed at the visitor, rather than at the needs of the attraction or the collection.

Education

The vast majority of attractions, particularly in the heritage area, would cite education as being the primary purpose behind their interpretation techniques. Education is actually much broader than being able to cater for the needs of school and college visits or even for groups of overseas tourists. Education should be taken in the broadest possible sense – in other words to educate the visitor, regardless of their age, gender or background. Essentially, this means conveying information in the most appropriate manner to cater for the widest possible range of visitors. Some key areas of the attraction may be specifically designed to educate younger visitors, while more complex information needs to be available alongside this. These interpretation techniques are for the wider visitor audience.

Research tip

For an example of an extensive section on educational goals and objectives which have been identified by a museum, visit the Education section of the Natural History Museum's website at www.nhm.ac.uk.

Entertainment

The second major area is to entertain. This is another very broad purpose and should not be purely applied to visitor attractions that are specifically designed for entertainment purposes, like theme parks. Museums, parks and historic sites aim to entertain, but not in exactly the same way as a theme park. Nevertheless, they seek to ensure that the visitor experience is an enjoyable and entertaining one. This may mean choosing interpretation techniques that give the visitor a taste of the attraction, its history and any characters that may be associated with it. Supplementary interpretation techniques, which breathe life into what could otherwise be a very passive experience for the visitor, are designed to convey information and ideas through entertainment.

> **Think**   Explore the Natural History Museum's website and find the Kids Only section. How appropriate are the entertainment features on the website? How many of them encourage visits? What age groups are catered for by the online selection of entertainment?

Figure 18.5 Education can also be entertaining

Example

Windsor Castle lies close to the river Thames to the west of London. It is an integral part of Windsor Great Park and a major tourist destination for both domestic and overseas visitors.

Figure 18.8 Map of Windsor

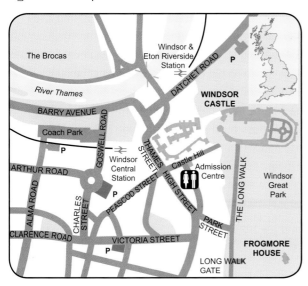

There are two conveniently located railway stations connecting Windsor with London Waterloo and Paddington. There are daily coach services from Victoria coach station in London and many tour companies operate daily excursions to the castle from major London hotels. The area is also accessible by the M4 and the M3 motorways.

Range of products and services provided

Every visitor attraction has its own unique range of primary, secondary and additional products and services. For many visitor attractions, the primary products and services offered are the key attractions that bring visitors to the site. All of the other products and services are supplementary. The secondary and additional products and services

aim to enhance the overall visitor experience. They offer alternative uses for the venue or provide necessary additional income or are related to accessibility and health and safety requirements.

Research tip

A quick way of identifying the range of products and services provided by a visitor attraction is to view their attraction map. Visit the Chester Zoo website at www.chesterzoo.org. Select 'Visitor Info', then select the 'Zoo Map' from the menu on the left.

Example

There is an enormous range of visitor attractions in the Norfolk Broads, ranging from windmills, churches, gardens, houses, nature reserves, theme parks and historic railways. In terms of primary, secondary and additional products and services, the range is varied. The major purpose of the Broads is the sailing and cruising holiday market. A large number of businesses focus on the provision of water-related leisure activities, including windsurfing, fishing, sailing and birdwatching.

Example

Windsor Castle is essentially an historic site, which covers 26 acres and incorporates a royal palace, a chapel and many other important buildings. It is also home to a large art collection and the world's most famous doll's house. The castle has sophisticated audio tours, guided tours and a range of themed products available in the on-site shops.

Cost of visiting

The cost of any visit to a visitor attraction must include not only any admission charges and necessary expenses while in the site itself, but also the cost of travelling to the attraction.
Some attractions have fixed admission charges, but they offer concessions for senior citizens, groups, children and students. They may offer free entry to particular groups, including the very young.

Some visitor attractions have special admission policies, such as the National Trust, which allows free entry to all of their sites for their members.

Research tip

Visit the website of the National Trust at www.nationaltrust.org.uk. By selecting 'Join' at the top of the home page, you will find a link showing the full membership benefits, which include free entry and parking at over 300 historic houses and gardens, plus other incentives.

Think Why do you think it might be advantageous for a visitor attraction to offer concessions to particular groups of visitors?

Example

There is no set admission charge for visiting the Norfolk Broads, although many of the individual attractions in the region do charge an entry fee. A prime example is Pleasurewood Hills Leisure Park (www.pleasurewoodhills.com) between Great Yarmouth and Lowestoft. The price of admission for visitors over 1.4 metres tall is £14.50. There are concessions for those under 1.4 metres, senior citizens, families, groups and school visitors. There are also discounts if tickets are purchased online.

Example

In 2007, the basic cost for admission to Windsor Castle for adults was £14.20. Family tickets offer a discount and children under the age of five are free. Residents of Windsor and Maidenhead that have an advantage card are allowed access to the castle free-of-charge. Concessions are also available for those over 60 years old and for students. Tickets can be purchased in advance, either online or by telephone, and group tickets also offer discounts.

Figure 18.9 Windsor Castle

Figure 18.10 Sailing on The Norfolk Broads

Image and novelty

An attraction's image is a blend of its status, purpose, marketing and popularity. Some visitor attractions have the advantage of having a strong image due to their historical importance or their reputation as a prime visitor attraction, such as Chessington World of Adventures or London Zoo. Others struggle to create an image for themselves and must rely on strong marketing and publicity in order to establish an image in the minds of potential visitors. With the enormous variety of visitor attractions in the UK, sites are no less competitive than retail outlets in terms of trying to attract customers.

The term novelty can also be applied to many visitor attractions and it suggests that they are unlike others or unique, therefore setting them apart from other visitor attractions in the immediate area. In a region associated with historic buildings, a theme park could be considered a novelty, whereas a historic building set in a region most closely associated with woodland or a natural environment has a novelty advantage.

Think Is there a visitor attraction that stands out as being novel in your local area, when compared to a range of very similar visitor attractions? Has this made the novel attraction more or less popular?

Example

The Norfolk Broads has a rather complex image. For some people, it is a centre for water sports and leisure activities, whereas for others it has a primary image of being a nature reserve and a wildlife centre. For some individuals, the image is more closely associated with man-made attractions such as Wroxham Barns, historic narrow gauge railways or Norwich Castle. Therefore, the area has a range of images for different groups of visitors. Due to the variety of different sites and activities in the area, it has more than one novelty factor.

Example

Windsor Castle has a unique image and novelty as it is closely associated with the Royal Family and has been a royal home for over 900 years. It still retains its purpose as a royal palace. It is one of a number of major historic buildings, including Sandringham in Norfolk, which has close associations with the Royal Family. The royal connection provides it not only with a clear image, but also sets it apart as having a distinct novelty compared to other competing historic buildings.

DIFFERENT TYPES OF VISITORS

Most visitor attractions try to appeal to the broadest possible range of customers, including adults, children, overseas visitors and groups. The attraction's ability to cater for these different types of visitors relies on the following key factors:

- Primary products and services — the nature of the exhibits and the basic purpose of the site

- Secondary and additional products and services – including shopping, tour guides, education and visitor services

- Interpretation techniques employed — this can determine whether the visitor attraction is appropriate for the widest possible range of visitors

- Purposes of the visitor interpretation, site and exhibits — this helps to frame the key objectives of the attraction and how it seeks to promote itself as a potential venue for customers to visit

- Appeal of the attraction — in terms of its accessibility and the range of products and services it offers

- Costs associated with visiting the attraction

- How the visitor attraction is perceived by potential visitors in terms of its image and its novelty value

Example

The wide range of different activities in the Norfolk Broads aims to cater for the very young, such as Pettitts Animal Adventure Park, to those interested in history, such as the Roman fort at Burgh Castle. Work is ongoing to improve accessibility for wheelchair users in and around the Broads area. The Norfolk Broads is a major centre for school visits and activities, organised by the Broads Authority itself.

Example

Windsor Castle is almost completely accessible for wheelchair users. The audio tours, guided tours and guidebooks are available in eight languages. The castle features free family activity trails and workshops and activities during school holidays.

CASE STUDY: FLAMINGO LAND

Flamingo Land is a theme park, zoo and holiday village that is situated in North Yorkshire. Cars and coaches can access it by using the A64 and it is also accessible by train, with Malton being the closest station. National Express and Yorkshire Coastliner coach services connect the attraction to York. The park is situated on the edge of the North Yorkshire Moors National Park, close to Scarborough. It is open daily and the admission cost is £20 for most visitors, although there are discounts available to older people, families, the disabled, groups and schools. There are a variety of rides, a substantial zoo, numerous daily entertainments and a number of cafes and restaurants at the attraction. The holiday village itself allows visitors to base their holidays in the area and this represents an additional source of income for the park. The park has a distinctive image, with the focus on entertainment, and it is the only combined theme park, zoo and holiday venue in the UK.

QUESTIONS

1. Using the Internet and the attraction's website www.flamingoland.co.uk, plan and cost a two-day visit to Flamingo Land from your area, considering travel costs to the attraction and overnight accommodation for one night.

2. Research the North Yorkshire Moors National Park area and identify three other attractions within an hour and a half's travelling distance of the park that would be appropriate for a group in the 16–20 age category.

Whenever a basic investment is made in the travel and tourism industry in a given area, jobs are created and other businesses are able to supply products and services, which in turn creates more jobs. The employees spend their wages in the local area, creating even more jobs. This process continues, but it is important to remember that the benefits of the multiplier effect only hold true if the majority of the money remains in the area. Foreign ownership of visitor attractions or visitor attractions that are owned by businesses based elsewhere in the country lead to leakages of money from the multiplier effect.

For example, in most developing countries, the leakage rate is between 40 and 80%. It is considerably less in more developed countries such as the UK.

> **Think** Certain resort areas in the UK are particularly affected by the success or failure of the resort and its attractions. Try to find at least one example of a previously popular resort that has lost its appeal and is suffering from high unemployment as a result.

Promoting cultural exchange

Many visitor attractions play another vital role in providing the opportunity for overseas visitors to experience a taste of UK culture, whether that is modern culture or from our historical past.

Visitor attractions also provide an opportunity for domestic tourists to experience the lives and histories of people from different regions of the country.

Example

In Great Yarmouth in Norfolk, there is a museum situated in a former herring smokehouse. Fishing was a vital part of the town's history for many years.

Example

Figure 18.12 Ironbridge foundry

In Shropshire at Ironbridge, there are many conserved factories and foundries from the early 19th century, which give both domestic and overseas tourists a taste of the UK's industrial past. These are all forms of cultural exchange and are not necessarily restricted purely to historic sites and museums.

Research tip

To find out more about the Time and Tide Museum in Great Yarmouth in the converted Victorian herring curing works, visit www.museums.norfolk.gov.uk and select the 'Time and Tide Museum' from the drop down menu.

Conservation

In a country such as the UK, which has a limited amount of space for new housing, commercial development and transport infrastructure, the preservation of important natural, heritage or cultural sites has taken on great importance. Conservation needs to be carefully balanced alongside the desire for particular areas or sites to attract visitors for educational, entertainment or purely profit-making purposes.

Example

The Eden Project in Cornwall is a prime example of conservation in action (www.edenproject.com). It has clear conservation, educational and science purposes and objectives.

In the past, many areas of extreme importance and buildings of immense historic interest were demolished or compromised as their value was not immediately recognised, or the site was simply not paying its way. This process has been reversed as new sources of funding have been found through grants and National Lottery payments. Certain areas and sites have also been able to attract funding from the European Union.

Example

Various local and countywide organisations have joined together to create a vision of how they see the future of Dorchester. It aims to address regeneration issues, along with continued contribution to the local economy, access to cultural sites and the protection of the Roman area of Dorchester and the more general conservation area.

In order to see the vision, the Dorchester Transport and Environment Plan (DTEP) created a zoned map, which illustrates the key areas that require specific improvement and development, as well as identifying gateways into the town centre and proposed pedestrian routes.

Figure 18.13 Aerial view of Dorchester

The key objectives of the new vision for Dorchester are:

*   increasing pedestrian priority and freedom;

*   protecting and enhancing the historic parts of the town;

*   reducing 'through traffic';

*   providing a better quality environment;

*   supporting the economic prosperity of the town;

*   ensuring access for emergency vehicles, servicing and public transport;

*   reduction of traffic speeds;

*   providing and improving access for cyclists, the elderly, the disabled, shoppers and residents.

Figure 18.14 Zoned map of the vision of Dorchester

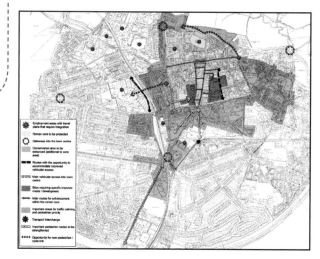

POPULARITY AND APPEAL

The ultimate measure of the importance and contribution of visitor attractions to a specific tourist destination is the number of visitors it actually attracts. The calculations are considerably more sophisticated than this, as they are measured not just in terms of the number of visitors. They are also counted and assessed in terms of the range of different types of visitors (including domestic and overseas, as well as groups, ages, gender, and cultural background).

The length of stay of the visitors is more important to the region as a whole. Towns, cities or regions that have a number of key visitor attractions are more likely to attract visitors that stay for longer periods of time. The longer the visitors stay in a specific area, the greater the impact in financial terms, as well as demands on local services and on the infrastructure. Jobs are created directly and indirectly through a variety of supporting, ancillary and other services and businesses in the area, including transport providers, restaurants, retail outlets and banks and building societies.

Example

According to the latest figures for Dorset, visitor spending is worth around £2 billion to the county annually. 65% of this total could be considered as direct spending on travel and tourism and the remainder is the indirect expenditure within the county. Over 50,000 actual jobs are supported by the travel and tourism industry. Visitors staying in the Dorset area spend almost £35 per person per day, with over 40% of this figure on accommodation. The other significant spending is on food and drink and shopping. These percentages have changed very little in the past 10 years. Nearly 70% of all visitors move around the area using their own transport. Just over 20% of visitors to Dorset are motivated by cultural, literary or heritage reasons. The main reason for visiting the county was the seaside at 46%. Just over 50% of all visitors travel in a group containing at least 2 adults. Around 55% of visitors

were staying in the county for at least 14 days and around 16% for at least 8 days. The vast majority of non-Dorset visitors come from the southwest of England. The other two major significant domestic tourist sources are the southeast and London. Overseas visitors account for barely 5%. On average, tourists visit 1 to 5 different visitor attractions (25%), while just over 30% visit between 6 and 10 visitor attractions. The majority of the tourists find out about potential attractions in Dorset either by brochures or on the Internet.

Figure 18.15 A busy Dorset beach

EVIDENCE ACTIVITY

P4 – M3 – D2

The council is impressed with the research that you have carried out so far. It has recently discovered that the Department for Culture, Media and Sport is offering significant grants to local councils if they can identify why tourism is important to their area in the context of UK tourism itself. In order to attract the grant, which should fund further research and considerably assist the local area in the development of its tourism, you have been asked to answer the following questions:

- Why it is important for the UK to attract visitors from overseas? (P4)

- Why it is important to attract domestic tourists from other parts of the country into your area? (P4)

- How can visitors coming to the area assist with regeneration? (P4)

- How does tourism contribute to both the national and the local economy? (P4)

- Why is it important to promote cultural exchange? (P4)

- How can tourism actually prove to be positive rather than negative in terms of conservation? (P4)

You should try to give national examples of visitor attractions that provide positive evidence on all of these points.

In addition, you are required to:

- provide national and local visitor numbers (P4);

- break these figures down by visitor type and length of stay (P4).

As the second part of the proposal to the government department, you now need to focus on your own town, city or region. You will have to refer to a minimum of three visitor attractions. This additional information is required by the department in order to help them make their decision about the awarding of the grants.

- How has tourism affected your area over the past three years? (M3)

- Provide figures about numbers of visitors and their spending. (M3)

- How have the attractions had an impact on the popularity and appeal of the area itself? (M3)

As the final part of the department's requirements, you need to make a critical evaluation of three named visitor attractions in your chosen area. This should provide the department with sufficient evidence that there is still considerable development work required in order for the attractions to reach their full potential.

- Using your own research or data that has already been collected, demonstrate the success so far of the attractions in contributing to the popularity and appeal of your area. (D2)

- Make any suitable recommendations as to how the improvement of the attractions would have a positive impact on the popularity and appeal of the area. Make sure that you justify your recommendations. (D2)

Hospitality Operations in Travel and Tourism

unit 19

Hospitality is an important element of the travel and tourism industry. In this unit, you will look at the products and services that are offered by different hospitality providers. This will include how food and beverage provision has become important to travel and tourism providers, either to differentiate their products – for example, an airline might have a better reputation for nicer food than its competition – or to increase expenditure at an attraction – for example, theme parks offer food and beverage provision so that customers will spend more money in the attraction.

You will also look at how hospitality providers aim to meet their customers' expectations and what these expectations are.

You will also develop your ability to plan hospitality provision by being creative and demonstrating your understanding of what customers' expectations are. You will look at factors that affect hospitality both internally and externally and consider how this will affect your plan.

By the end of this unit, you will:

So you want to be a...

Conference and Banqueting Manager

My name James Cooper

Age 31

Income £21,000 + benefits

If you enjoy planning and organising, can keep your cool and make quick decisions, you'll love this job!

What do you do?

I'm the conference and banqueting manager for a middle-sized (60 rooms) hotel which is part of a national chain of hotels.

What responsibilities do you have?

I'm responsible for the organisation and running of conferences and banquets within the hotel. I also have responsibility for the budget for my department as well as a remit to increase sales.

How did you get into the job?

Well I left college in 1995 with a BTEC National Diploma in Travel and Tourism. As part of the course we had to plan and run an event, which I just loved doing. So when I left college I applied to all the hotels, conference and exhibition centres across the Midlands. I started working at a small, local hotel in Dudley as a conference supervisor, which was a huge learning curve.

How did you find your current job?

It was advertised in the back of The Hotelkeeper and Caterer magazine. I'd known this hotel for a number of years as I grew up in this area.

What training did you get?

Over the years I've had a number of training courses on everything from customer service to health and safety. I've developed most of my skills over time and through experience, but without the knowledge I got from my BTEC National Diploma I wouldn't have known where to start.

What are the hours like?

The hours can be a bit long and antisocial, especially in spring and summer when we do so many weddings.

> **Many of the events can be quite exciting**

What skills do you need?

You need to be organised to do my job. You also need to be a quick thinker and a good problem solver. Interpersonal skills are important, as are selling skills.

How good is the pay?

The pay is good, but I do work hard for it. The company has just started to introduce an element of performance-related pay. I do get a few tips from time to time.

What about the future?

At the moment I'm happy with what I'm doing. Although I am considering reducing my hours so that I can spend more time with my family – I've got two boys .

Grading criteria

The table below shows what you need to do to gain a pass, merit or distinction in this part of the qualification. Make sure you refer back to it when you are completing work so that you can judge whether you are meeting the criteria and what you need to do to fill in gaps in your knowledge or experience.

In this unit there are 3 evidence activities that give you an opportunity to demonstrate your achievement of the grading criteria:

page 151   P1

page 157   P1, P2, M1, D1

page 169   P3, P4, M2, M3, D2

To achieve a pass grade the evidence must show that the learner is able to...	To achieve a merit grade the evidence must show that, in addition to the pass criteria, the learner is able to...	To achieve a distinction grade the evidence must show that, in addition to the pass and merit criteria, the learner is able to...
P1 Describe the products and services involved within different types of hospitality provision	**M1** Compare how two selected hospitality providers meet the expectations of different types of customers through the provision of products and services	**D1** Recommend improvements to the products and services provided by a selected hospitality provider
P2 Explain how hospitality providers meet the expectations of three different types of customers	**M2** Explain how their plan for hospitality provision meets the needs of the travel and tourism organisation's objectives and its customers	**D2** Analyse how internal and external factors may affect the success of the planned hospitality provision in a travel and tourism organisation.
P3 Plan hospitality provision for a travel and tourism organisation	**M3** Assess how hospitality operations in travel and tourism organisations have responded to internal and external factors.	
P4 Explain how three internal and three external factors affect hospitality operations in travel and tourism organisations.		

19.1 *Know the products and services offered by different types of hospitality provision*

The hospitality sector of the travel and tourism industry is one of the major sectors of the industry with over 1.6 million of the 2.1 million people employed in travel and tourism working in it. There are a diverse number of establishments in the hospitality sector.

The hospitality sector of travel and tourism can be split into two different parts: providers where hospitality is the main business and providers where hospitality is an additional service.

Table 19.1 Distribution of jobs in the hospitality industry 2002

Hotels	279,785
Restaurants	508,483
Pubs, clubs and bars	261,130
Contract catering	192,298
Total hospitality businesses	1,241,696
Hospitality services	304,187
Total main jobs	1,545,883
Second job in hospitality	121,109
Total UK hospitality industry	1,666,992

HOSPITALITY PROVIDERS AS A MAIN BUSINESS

These are organisations where the provision of accommodation, food and drink are offered as the main business. We will look at the main types of business in this part of the hospitality industry. The boundaries between different types of businesses are not always clearly defined. This is mainly due to the fact that businesses can diversify into any area where the management sees that there is an opportunity.

Hotels

Hotels are organisations whose main business is the provision of accommodation, food and drink. Hotels in the UK can be categorised into a number of different sub-groups with clearly defined differences:

- Town house hotels — small hotels situated in towns that specialise in the provision of a high standard of accommodation and food and drink, but tend to have a small number of rooms.

- Country house hotels — the country cousins to the town house hotel, usually offering high standards of provision and quite often offering countryside pursuits or leisure facilities.

- Budget hotels — offering a limited basic service for a limited price. This has been a big growth area in accommodation and includes some large companies like Premier Travel Inn and Travelodge.

- Hotel groups and consortia — large groups of hotels offering provision at a number of different locations across the country and the world. These include companies like Best Western and Holiday Inn.

Figure 19.1 Holiday Inn hotels can be found in many countries

Guesthouses

The guesthouses category also includes bed and breakfasts and inns. They tend to be privately-owned establishments that may have just one room and certainly no more than ten rooms. Guesthouses generally offer cheaper accommodation than hotels. The service tends to be more homely as you are being welcomed into someone's house as a guest.

Holiday centres

Holiday centres started in 1936 when Billy Butlin opened his first holiday camp at Skegness called Butlin's. Holiday camps reached their peak in the late 1960s and early 1970s when cheap flights and holidays started to compete with the holiday camps. Holiday centres have undergone a dramatic change in recent years. Holiday camps like Butlin's were obliged to reinvent themselves and change their provision to suit modern-day consumers.

There has also been a growth in all-inclusive holidays. These are package holidays where all food, drink and accommodation are provided in the price.

Figure 19.2 Butlin's logo

Example

When you book a holiday with the all-inclusive Caribbean specialist, Beaches, you can expect your holiday to include all meals, drinks, scuba diving, sailing and even entertainment.

Figure 19.3 An example of a purpose-built caravan site

Think What kinds of customers would be attracted to holiday centres like Butlin's? Who would be drawn to a Beaches holiday?

Campsites

The UK is the birthplace of camping. It is a value for money holiday with site prices as low as £5 per night for a pitch. Many campsites in the UK have pitches with running water, drainage and electricity. Although at many sites you need to provide your own tent, there are also some sites where tents can be hired for the night.

Some campsites also welcome touring vehicles including motor homes and caravans. Shops, restaurants and entertainment are provided on some sites, as well as shower and toilet facilities.

Caravan parks

Caravan parks may offer you a space for your own caravan or the hire of static caravans. This is another cost-effective way of going on holiday, but it allows for a few more home comforts than camping.

Research tip

Use the Internet to find out about caravan parks in your local area. Find out how much it costs if you use your own caravan or to hire a static caravan.

HOSPITALITY PROVIDERS AS AN ADDITIONAL SERVICE

A number of organisations offer hospitality as an additional service. This is because they can either increase charges for a service or generate additional expenditure by offering a hospitality service.

Airlines offer food and drink to customers on flights. Budget airlines normally charge for this as an additional service. Charter and scheduled airlines provide food and drink as part of the product. A business class passenger can expect a better range of food and beverages than a standard class passenger.

Almost all airlines have on board duty free goods such as fragrances, alcohol and other products that passengers can purchase at lower prices than those offered by high street stores.

Figure 19.4 Carriage House Restaurant, Chatsworth House

Conferences and exhibitions

Food and drinks are offered to customers who are holding conferences and exhibitions as refreshments. From the provider's perspective, this also gives them the opportunity to increase the peripheral spend. Accommodation can also be provided for conferences and exhibitions as some delegates may have to travel a long distance in order to attend.

> **Think** Can you think of any other services that conference delegates might need?

Attractions

Attractions also offer food and drinks to their customers. This is to increase the average expenditure at the attraction, but it also has the benefit of letting the customers have a longer dwell time. The provision of food and drinks is usually in keeping with the attraction. For example, a tearoom is a common hospitality provision at a stately home.

Example

Chatsworth House in Derbyshire has the Farmyard Café and the Carriage House Restaurant, both of which offer local, home-cooked snacks and meals in environments that are in keeping with the stately home.

Key words

Peripheral spend — money spent by the customer, but not on the core product
Dwell time — the amount of time that a customer spends at an attraction

Research tip

Think of a local tourist attraction in your area. Use leaflets and the Internet to find out about the hospitality provision that it offers.

CORE PRODUCTS AND SERVICES

There are three core provisions of the hospitality sector: food, drink and accommodation.

Food

The range of food on offer in the UK is vast, ranging from fast food and coffee shops to some of the world's best restaurants. London has the second largest number of Michelin star restaurants of any city in the world. The UK's multicultural society has led to a wide range of ethnic cuisine from European neighbours like France and Spain to more diverse tastes such as Thai and Chinese. Given this extensive range of cuisine, the most important aspect is to offer the customer what they want to eat at a price that they perceive to be value for money.

Drink

The range of drink (or beverage) provision available in the UK is as diverse as its food choices. The traditional drink provision in the UK was hotel bars, public houses and tearooms. In recent years, there has been a decline in the number of traditional public houses. However, there has been a massive growth in the number of coffee shops and juice bars since the late 1990s. This coincides with the changing consumer behaviour from a pub culture to a café culture and a move towards a healthier lifestyle.

Figure 19.5 Tents on a campsite are a low-budget option

Accommodation

Like the range of food and beverage provision, the variety of accommodation on offer in the UK is also extremely diverse. Prices range from £5 per night for a pitch on a campsite to thousands of pounds for a suite at a 5-star hotel.

Figure 19.6 A luxury hotel suite

So you want to be ...

Cabin crew

My name Claire Anderson
Age 21
Income £12,500

If you're friendly, able to keep calm in a crisis and enjoy teamwork, this could be the job for you...

What do you do?

My main role is to ensure the safety of passengers, but I also look after passengers by providing customer care on board the aircraft.

What responsibilities do you have?

I make sure the aircraft is ready to board, greet passengers and help them to their seat. I prepare the aircraft for departure and perform the safety demonstration. I sort out passenger problems, sell a range of goods from the in-flight brochure and offer a drinks and meals service. Prior to arrival, I make sure safety regulations are complied with, passengers are in their seats with seat belts fastened, aisles are clear and overhead lockers are secure. Once we land, I help the passengers disembark the aircraft and prepare the aircraft for the next departure.

How did you get into the job?

I have a BTEC National Diploma in Travel and Tourism and I started applying for cabin crew positions when I was 18.

How did you find your current job?

Most airlines have websites and I applied online when I was at college. It is worth spending a lot of time on your application because competition is really tough.

> ❝ **Competition [for jobs] is really tough** ❞

What training did you get?

I did four weeks at the airline training school before I was allowed to fly. During that time we learnt about safety and airline policies and procedures. It involved being in a smoke-filled chamber, which was really scary, and time in a swimming pool helping pretend passengers climb into an inflatable life raft.

What are the hours like?

Unsociable! Sometimes I have to be at the airport for 0400 hours.

What skills do you need?

You need to be friendly, and diplomatic. As cabin crew, you work in a team so you need to be a good team worker and communicator. You need to be smart and tidy and having a good level of education is becoming more and more important. Finally, you have to be fit and well as it is not easy working at 35,000 feet.

How good is the pay?

I started on £10,000 three years ago and I now earn £12,500. The best companies to work for are the scheduled airlines as they pay the best rates.

What about the future?

I am starting to think about my next job. I'd like to work in the marketing department of an airline.

Grading criteria

The table below shows what you need to do to gain a pass, merit or distinction in this part of the qualification. Make sure you refer back to it when you are completing work so that you can judge whether you are meeting the criteria and what you need to do to fill in gaps in your knowledge or experience.

In this unit there are 4 evidence activities that give you an opportunity to demonstrate your achievement of the grading criteria:

page 177   P1

page 187   P2, M1, D1

page 193   P3, P4, M2

page 196   P5, M3, D2

To achieve a pass grade the evidence must show that the learner is able to...	To achieve a merit grade the evidence must show that, in addition to the pass criteria, the learner is able to...	To achieve a distinction grade the evidence must show that, in addition to the pass and merit criteria, the learner is able to...
P1 Describe the options available to customers when travelling to and from airports and between terminals	**M1** Compare the facilities available at two different airports for passengers travelling to and from the airports and during the embarkation process	**D1** Evaluate the effectiveness of processes for handling passengers during embarkation at a specific airport, making justified recommendations for improvement
P2 Describe the process for embarkation for all passengers and the role that airport and airline staff have during the embarkation of customer	**M2** Explain the importance of providing facilities to meet specific passenger needs both onboard and during the boarding process	**D2** Analyse the effectiveness of disembarkation processes at a UK airport.
P3 Describe the boarding process	**M3** Explain the importance of effective disembarkation processes at UK airports.	
P4 Describe the role of staff and the facilities available for customers during a flight		
P5 Describe the disembarkation and transit processes at UK airports.		

24.1 *Know the options available to customers when travelling to and from airports*

TRANSPORT

Major road and rail networks

While travelling by car is the preferred option of many passengers, particularly those travelling for leisure purposes, it is the least favoured by airports. Cars cause road congestion near to the airport and car parking is costly to provide, as well as using up valuable land that may be needed for essential operational activities. Many airports are actively pursuing policies to dissuade passengers from using cars, such as high car parking charges, and providing alternative means of access.

Many train connections exist between major airports and urban centres. However, rail services sometimes only run at certain times of the day and may not be available at night-time.

Example

The Heathrow Express is a dedicated rail link that operates a non-stop rail service for air passengers between Central London (Paddington) and Heathrow Airport.

Coach services

Many airports have interconnecting coach services at reasonable prices, leaving from a major transport hub and arriving just in front of the terminal.

Example

Terravision is a privately-run coach service with business throughout Europe. One of its most used routes is from London Victoria Coach Station to Stansted Airport.

Taxis and private hire

Many airports have a taxi rank just outside the terminal building. These companies may offer competitive set prices for certain distances or destinations. At the very least, most airports have a phone that connects straight through to a taxi service.

Think How does your nearest airport dissuade passengers from using cars to travel to and from the airport?

This is Marco Polo Airport in Venice. If you look to the front and bottom left, you can see the public water buses and water taxis that take air passengers between the airport and Venice city centre. While water buses and taxis are among the more unusual forms of transport to/from an airport, they are extremely popular with the many tourists visiting Venice.

Figure 24.1 Marco Polo Airport, Venice

CAR PARKING

Passengers travelling by car to the airport and parking their car there until they return will normally have several car parking options. The larger the airport, the more options are available. These may include:

- airport short-stay car parks;

- airport long-stay car parks;

- off-airport car parks operated by the airport;

- off-airport car parks operated by private companies;

- airline car parks for business/first class passengers;

- a VIP car park.

Airport long-stay and off-airport car parks are normally located too far away from the passenger terminal for passengers to walk, especially if they have baggage. To overcome this problem, the operators run regular courtesy coach services that transfer passengers and their baggage between the car park and the passenger terminal. A small VIP car park is usually located close to the terminal.

Example

At Manchester Airport, there are a variety of car parking options which are priced according to their closeness to the terminal. Shuttle Park offers a courtesy bus service, takes 15 minutes to arrive at the terminal and costs the least. Short Stay is parking just below the terminal and costs considerably more.

INTER-TERMINAL TRANSPORT

When airports reach a certain size, they tend to expand by building another passenger terminal and splitting their traffic between the terminals. The split in traffic will vary according to the type of airport, but the most commonly used methods are by airline, route or a combination of both, such as British Airways Terminal or **Domestic** Terminal.

Passengers flying into airports may end their journey at that airport or use the airport to fly out to another destination. Passengers flying out to another destination without breaking their journey are either **transfer** or **transit passengers**.

A transit passenger might remain on their aircraft or be taken into the terminal, but they will remain **airside**. Major airports will generally have a transit lounge available for their use.

Example

A typical transit passenger would be a passenger travelling between London Heathrow and Sydney Airport in Australia with a two-hour re-fuelling stop at Singapore (Changi) Airport. During the re-fuelling stop, passengers are disembarked into the transit lounge at Singapore.

Think Have you or any of your friends or family been transit passengers?

Key words

Domestic – travelling within the UK
Transfer passengers – passengers flying into the airport on one aircraft and departing on a second aircraft without breaking his or her journey
Transit passengers – passengers flying into and departing from the airport in the same aircraft, which stops to pick up additional passengers and/or cargo and/or to re-fuel
Airside – the security controlled area of the airport that are only available to air passengers and staff

PERSONNEL AND STAFF ROLES

The aviation industry employs a significant number of staff. An airport with 10 million passengers is typically supported by approximately 30,000 staff. Many are involved in passenger-handling functions, while others are involved in support functions both on and off the airport. The jobs all these staff do are far too numerous to mention individually, but it is worth considering some of the key staff employed in ensuring that passengers and aircraft are processed safely and efficiently.

Airport staff

Key airport staff include terminal duty managers, information desk staff, porters, and marshalers. Perhaps the most important role at the airport is the Terminal Duty Manager as he/she is responsible for liaising, coordinating and controlling all of the on-airport activities to ensure the airport runs as smoothly as possible. This critical role is usually undertaken by an experienced aviation person who has spent several years in a customer service role for an airport, airline or handling agent. Candidates for this job are normally educated to degree level, possess good customer service skills, are excellent communicators and have the ability to interpret information and prioritise. In addition to liaising with the numerous organisations based at the airport, they are also responsible for leading the team of airport staff. If something goes wrong at the airport, it is the Terminal Duty Manager who has to sort it out. The term 'duty' means that the post is continuous with one Terminal Duty Manager taking over from another on a continuous 24 hours per day, 7 days per week basis.

Information desk staff provide information to passengers and other airport users to ease their way through airport systems and procedures. Airport porters collect and organise baggage trolleys, assist passengers with their baggage and provide help for passengers with special needs. Marshalers perform a key airside safety role by guiding aircraft to their **stand** and inspecting the **apron**, **taxiways** and runways to ensure they are safe and all regulations are being complied with by airlines and other organisations.

> ### Key words
> **Stand** – designated parking place for aircraft
> **Apron** – large expanse of concrete where aircraft park and manoeuvre in front of the passenger terminal. Sometimes called the ramp.
> **Taxiways** – roads for aircraft that join key aircraft operational areas, the apron and runway

Airline staff

Key airline staff include ticket sales staff, flight crew, cabin crew and engineering staff. Ticket sales staff have become less important with the advent of e-ticketing, but staff are still needed at airports to sell, exchange or refund tickets. Flight crew are responsible for piloting the aircraft. Cabin crew have an important passenger safety role and engineers are responsible for maintaining and servicing aircraft.

Control authorities

Every point of arrival to or departure from the UK is monitored by the control authorities. These are government organisations which check that people, baggage and freight coming into or leaving the UK comply with regulations on health, security and immigration. They also ensure that restricted or prohibited goods are not being smuggled into or out of the country.

HM Revenue and Customs

HM Revenue and Customs was formed in 2005 following the merger of the Inland Revenue and HM Customs and Excise departments. The department has a wide remit, collecting numerous taxes, including income tax, VAT, child benefit and recovery of student loans.

At an airport, the main roles of HM Revenue and Customs are:

- to detect the illegal importation or exportation of drugs, obscene and indecent material and endangered species;

- to check that passengers from non-EU countries are not bringing in more than their duty free allowance;

- to inspect cargo and check documentation of freight to ensure they comply with export and import procedures.

Immigration and Nationality Directorate (IND)

The Immigration and Nationality Directorate is part of the Home Office and its purpose is to regulate entry to and settlement in the UK, in the interests of sustainable growth and social inclusion.

If you are a returning UK citizen, a visitor to the UK, someone wishing to remain or settle in the UK or an asylum seeker, you will come into contact with IND. The IND's most visible face is the Immigration Service, which operates at ports and airports.

The Police/Special Branch

Police officers, usually armed, patrol the airport in the same way as they would patrol a small town. Apart from everyday crimes, they have to be alert to any possible terrorist activity.

Special Branch has an overt and covert presence at airports. Overtly, they have a manned entry point in the Common Travel Area and in Domestic Arrivals for certain flights. Covertly, they often work with the other control authorities to track and apprehend criminals and terrorists.

Port Health

Every airport has to ensure that passengers carrying infectious diseases do not enter the UK. This work is the responsibility of the Public Health Laboratory Service (PHLS), which is part of the NHS. The PHLS protects the population from infection by working to control and prevent the spread of infectious diseases. It helps infected patients by identifying the organism that is causing the disease and by providing expert advice and treatment. PHLS also check the paperwork of aircraft to make sure that the aircraft have been sprayed to destroy any possible source of contamination.

Ground handlers and customer service staff

Handling agent staff, such as customer service agents, are responsible for passenger check-in, embarkation and disembarkation. Apron hands load and unload baggage and provide other services for aircraft.

Security staff

Air traffic controllers and security staff may be directly employed by the airport or contracted by the airport. Air traffic controllers guide aircraft through corridors in the sky and ensure they land and take off safely. Security staff perform a number of vital functions, such as patrolling the airport perimeter fence, controlling traffic outside the terminal, and searching passengers, baggage and aircraft.

EVIDENCE ACTIVITY

P2 – M1 – D1

For P2, with an airport you are familiar with, draw a flow chart of the embarkation procedures and comment on what happens at each stage, paying particular attention to passengers with special needs. At the appropriate point, draw a separate flow chart for baggage. Here is an example of a flow chart.

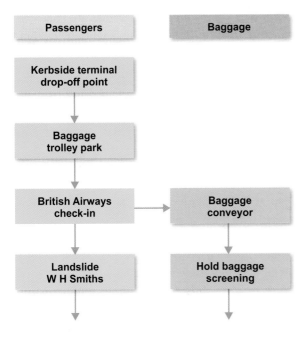

Choose at least one of the staff roles from the categories mentioned and research:

a) job entry requirements, qualifications, experience and personal qualities required to undertake the role;

b) job description and a summary of the post holder's duties;

c) career progression – for example, a career in Air Traffic Control (ATC) normally involves candidates starting as an Air Traffic Control Assistant before qualifying to undertake the role of Air Traffic Control Officer. Management roles in ATC include team leaders on a duty roster basis and a Senior Air Traffic Control Officer in overall charge of ATC at an airport.

On your flow chart, indicate where key airport and airline staff are involved and comment on their roles during the passenger embarkation process. Here is an example of a flow chart.

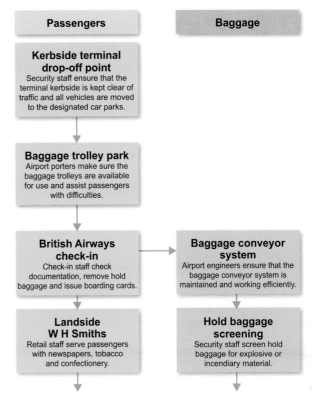

M1 asks you to compare the facilities available at two different airports for passengers travelling to and from the airports. You should have collected this information during 24.1, so at this point you only need to comment on the information and indicate any differences. To complete M1, you need to compare the flow chart exercise with the embarkation process at another airport. If you were to compare Manchester Airport with a smaller airport such as Leeds Bradford, you would notice that Manchester Airport has more facilities and services.

For D1, evaluate the effectiveness of procedures for handling air passengers during embarkation and disembarkation at a specific airport, making justified recommendations for improvement. (You may ignore the disembarkation part as D2 asks you to do the same.) Examine the flow chart of your chosen airport and evaluate the effectiveness of the procedures and make recommendations. For example, perhaps it is not easy to board passengers and the process could be improved by installing air bridges. This can be justified on the basis that customer service is improved, passengers with mobility problems can access the aircraft far more easily and the boarding process is much quicker.

24.3 *Know the facilities and services available to passengers during the flight*

BOARDING

Passengers in the departure lounge are expected to watch the flight information monitors for the 'go to gate' message and they should then make their way down the pier to the gate lounge.

> ### Key words
>
> Gate – passengers leave the terminal to board their aircraft through a gate. At small airports, this may be nothing more than a number above a departure lounge exit door. At large airports, passengers often walk or use travellators from the departure lounge to a forward gate lounge that is situated next to the aircraft stand.
>
> Pier – a long, thin building protruding from the departure lounge out onto the apron area. The purpose of the pier is to bring passengers and their aircraft closer together. The inside of the pier contains walkways, travellators and gate lounges.

Preferential seating and cabin baggage

An announcement asks passengers to board the flight. Special needs passengers and people with small children are boarded first. Some airlines offer preferential seating for passengers who have paid either to be seated first or for a different class. The ground crew then calls other passengers to board according to seat numbers. As passengers pass through the gate controls, passports are checked against boarding cards. Special attention is given to the destination on the boarding card to make sure that passengers are boarding the correct flight. When onboard, cabin crew assist passengers in stowing their cabin luggage in the panels above or under the seat in front.

Security checks

When there is heightened security, it is not unusual for additional searches of passengers and carry-on baggage to take place as passengers leave the gate lounge to board their aircraft.

Figure 24.6 Passports are checked as passengers go through gate controls

Figure 24.8 The pilot and co-pilot discuss flight plans

Giving information

Before take-off, cabin crew are required by law to provide a safety demonstration about the various procedures in the case of an emergency on board.

Managing passenger behaviour

Cabin crew are fully versed in passenger management, such as resolving seating arrangement issues and disagreements between passengers. They also care for passengers with special needs and hand out immigration forms, making sure that passengers comply with procedures. So-called air rage is on the increase and cabin crew may be put at risk from physically violent or verbally abusive passengers.

> ***Think*** What do you think causes passengers to behave in this way and what can airlines do to try and prevent such occurrences happening in the future?

Sale of goods, food and beverages

Cabin crew also have the job of selling tax- and duty-free goods and providing in-flight meals, snacks and drinks.

EVIDENCE ACTIVITY

P3 – P4 – M2

For P3, continue with your flow chart to include the boarding process. Describe what happens at each stage.

For P4, you need to use the evidence collected in this section and describe the role of staff and the facilities available for passengers during a flight.

M2 asks you to explain the importance of providing facilities to meet specific passenger needs both on board and during the boarding process. You might like to base your answer around the information collected from British Airways.

Figure 24.9 Onboard safety demonstration

24.4 Know the airport and airline services and facilities during the disembarkation process

Once the aircraft has landed, taxied to the gate and come to a halt, the disembarkation process begins. Disembarkation is similar to embarkation only in reverse and on these occasions, passengers with mobility problems are the last to leave the aircraft as they have to wait for assistance to arrive.

PASSPORT AND VISA REQUIREMENTS

General immigration procedures

Once passengers are inside the terminal, their first port of call is immigration. This process can be extremely quick if the flight is between two European Union (EU) countries and the Immigration Officer may not even attend.

Non-EU passengers enter through a different channel and are subjected to different levels of scrutiny, depending on their point of origin and/or their nationality status. The process involving non-EU passengers usually commences with filling out a boarding card in-flight and checking passports, visas or other entry documentation at the immigration control.

Procedures for asylum seekers

For asylum seekers entering the UK without a passport as they are fleeing from persecution in their homeland, the process is long-winded. The Government is attempting to introduce new measures including the x-raying of teeth and bones to establish the age of asylum seekers.

Validity requirements for EU passport holders and visas

UK and other EU citizens travelling outside the EU may be subjected to a variety of requirements in terms of passports and their length of remaining validity, visas and medical certificates. This process can be protracted even further by security checks at immigration. For example, a UK citizen travelling into the US for leisure purposes may have to have a retina scan.

Research tip

Go to the US Embassy site and check the entry requirements into the US for a UK citizen on a two-week holiday, and a six-month work placement student studying travel and tourism.

Customs

Before entering the destination country, passengers are required to pass through customs. In European Union countries, there are normally three customs channels: the green 'nothing to declare', the red 'goods to declare' and the blue 'Arrivals from the European Union' channels. If passengers are arriving from outside the EU, they have to choose which channel to pass through. Customs personnel watch the passengers thoroughly and can stop anyone they consider to be suspicious. They are authorised to exercise customs duties if passengers are in excess of their legal import limits and to remove items if they are restricted or banned in the arrival country.

Research tip

Go to the HM Revenue and Customs website and find out information on tax- and duty-free allowances from non-EU countries, recommended limits for EU countries and restricted and prohibited items.

Edexcel
190 High Holborn
London WC1V 7BH

© Edexcel 2008

The rights of Jon Sutherland, Diane Sutherland, Carol Spencer, Andy Kerr, Victoria Lindsay and Derek Brickell to be identified as authors of this Work have been asserted by them in accordance with the Copyright, Designs and Patents Act, 1988.

ISBN: 978-1-40586-809-9

Printed and bound in China SWTC/01
Illustration by Oxford Designers & Illustrators Ltd
Indexed by Richard Howard

Acknowledgments
The Publisher is grateful to the following for their permission to reproduce copyright material:

CAA for data from the 2006 tables "Busiest UK airports" and "Activity at UK airports" Civil Aviation Authority and UK Airport Statistics copyright © Civil Aviation Authority 2006, reprinted with permission; Department of Transport for the tables "Forecast terminal passenger numbers at UK airport 1998 to 2020 (m)" and "Forecast passenger numbers in the domestic market (m)" published on www.dft.gov. uk Crown copyright 2007; DSA for data and information about The Driving Standards Agency (DSE) published on www.dsa.gov.uk Crown copyright 2007; First Choice Holidays for an extract about First Choice jobs published on www.firstchoice4jobs.co.uk and First Choice Holiday Kids' Clubs published on www.firstchoice.co.uk copyright © First Choice, reprinted with permission; The Independent News & Media Ltd for an extract adapted from "Airline Passenger Jailed for Bomb Joke" published in The Independent 22nd February 2006 copyright © The Independent 2006; Manchester Airport for the Manchester Airport Coach Network Plan published on www.manchesterairport.co.uk copyright © Manchester Airport plc, All rights reserved, reprinted with permission; Neilson Active Holidays Limited for an extract about ski representatives published on www.neilson.co.uk copyright © Neilson Active Holidays, reprinted with permission; Sea Cloud Cruises GmbH for an extract from Sea Cloud II daily itinerary 3rd July 2003, Noble Caledonia Prospect Tours(Helsinki, Finland) copyright © Sea Cloud Cruises 2003; Stagecoach Supertram for the Sheffield Supertram Route Map published on www.supertram.com copyright © Stagecoach Supertram, reprinted with permission; and Thomas Cook Tour Operations Ltd for an extract from the Club 18-30 Guide, Summer 2007 © Thomas Cook.

Picture Credits
The publisher would like to thank the following for their kind permission to reproduce their photographs:

(Key: b-bottom; c-centre; l-left; r-right; t-top)

Alamy Images: Aardvark 150b; Richard Boot 82; Brother Luck 165; Gerard Brown 193t; Andrew Fox 167; Robert Fried 46; Jeff Greenberg 188; Imagebroker 193b; Justin Kase 94; Look Die Bildagentur der Fotograten 160; Neil McAllister 21; National Trust Photo Library 161; Pictures of London 179; Profimedia International 152; Scottish Viewpoint 51; Alex Segre 158; Adrian Sherratt 148; Shoesmith Windemere Collection 50; SlickShots 191; David Stares 92; Stockfolio 45; John Sturrock 163; Mark Wagner 170-171, 172; Rob Wells 147; Dave Wyatt Photography 116-117, 118; **Chatsworth House Trust:** 149; **Thomas Cook:** 60; **Corbis:** 27, 41, 144-145, 146, 150t, 175, 182, 183, 184; **DK Images:** 10-11, 12, 25, 34-5, 36, 38, 52, 56-57, 58, 84-85, 86, 121, 122, 132, 133, 139, 141, 173; **English Heritage:** 125, 126; **Gloucestershire County Council:** 127; **Robert Harding World Imagery:** 16; **Hilton Hotels:** 162; **Jenni Johns:** 15; **Metro, The West Yorkshire Passenger Transport Executive:** 91; **Neilson Active Holidays:** 61; **PA Photos:** 120, 153; **Pearson Education:** 11, 35, 57, 85, 117, 145, 171; **Rex Features:** 79, 102, 103; **Roger Scruton:** 47, 168; **Skyscan:** B Croxford 140; **Sunscape Yachting:** 43; **SuperStock:** 32; **Thomson Holidays:** 14, 19, 66, 78

Cover images: *Front:* **DK Images:** Cecile Treal & Jean Michel Ruiz

All other images © Pearson Education

Picture Research by Thelma Gilbert

Every effort has been made to trace the copyright holders and we apologise in advance for any unintentional omissions. We would be pleased to insert the appropriate acknowledgement in any subsequent edition of this publication.